Classic Marques

Vauxhall Cars
1965-1984

Alan Earnshaw & Robert W Berry

NOSTALGIA ROAD

First published by
Transpennine Publishing 2000
This edition Crécy Publishing Limited 2013

© Text: Alan Earnshaw & Robert W Berry 2000/2013
© Photographs: Vauxhall Motors Ltd
(All rights reserved)

All rights reserved. No part of this book may be reproduced or transmitted in any form or by any means electronic or mechanical, including photocopying, recording or by any information storage without permission from the Publisher in writing. All enquiries should be directed to the Publisher.

A CIP record for this book is available from the British Library

ISBN 9781908 347206

Printed in Malta by Melita Press

Nostalgia Road is an imprint of Crécy Publishing Limited
1a Ringway Trading Estate
Shadowmoss Road
Manchester M22 5LH
www.crecy.co.uk

Acknowledgements: This book is the work of a large number of individuals, but any errors or omissions are the sole responsibility of the authors. From start to finish the book was put together in just over ten weeks, in order for it to be launched originally at the Vauxhall, Bedford Opel Owners' gathering at the Billing Aquadrome, Northampton in July 2001.

Fortunately we have had the benefit of considerable experience and input from many Vauxhall owners, as well as access to the archives at Luton. Both Alan and myself drove Vauxhall cars, he a Zafira and myself a Vectra, so we were both very close to the subject. In addition we were also heavily involved in the restoration of four Bedford coaches, so this has been no arduous task, merely a labour of love.

Special thanks to all those who have helped in our project thus far, especially: John Ankerman; Ron Atkins; Mike Berry; Peter Blincow; Tony Burnip; Terry Calvert; Ray Cooper; Nigel Griggs; Stuart Harris; Barry Harvey; Bernard Ridgeley; Peter Stone; Louise Tarn; David Townend; David Turner; and, all those Vauxhall employees, dealers and enthusiasts who (over the years) helped make the marque what it is! RWB

Front Cover: Seen during publicity filming in Scotland, this superbly rustic scene captures a once familiar sight that is mostly forgotten by motorists of today. Here the driver of a 1964 FC Victor fills up with Esso five-star petrol.

Rear Cover Top: The sporty SRV car dated from 1966.

Rear Cover Bottom: Now for a much more modern Esso-Vauxhall picture, as a pre-production Brabham Viva HB is seen outside one of the new Esso Motor Lodge motels in 1966. The Brabham Viva was not really a serious motor sports contender but was more of a 'life-style' car. The car came on the market in 1967, and had a very distinctive 'sporty' livery. The primary schemes were white with a racing green flash, or racing green with a white flash. It also carried decals for the Brabham name and a pair of 'chequer flags'.

Contents Page: As moves were being made to standardise/internationalise the GM range, the so-called 'T-Car' programme was developed. Here in Britain the 'T-Car' was known as the Chevette, but on its launch in 1975 only a three-door model was offered; the four-door and the estate followed in 1976. So, whilst there are no less than 12 examples of the new model in this picture taken on 28 April 1975, all are original hatchbacks.

Contents

Introduction	4
Model Types	
HB Viva 1966-1970	10
FD Victor 1967-1972	17
HC Viva 1970-1979	23
Firenza 1971-1973	27
Firenza 'Droopsnoot' 1973-1975	29
Magnum 1973-1977	30
FE Victor, VX 1800 and VX2300 1972-1978	32
Cavalier 1975-1988	36
Chevette 1975-1984	42
Carlton 1978-1986	47
Royale 1978-1982	49
Viceroy 1980-1982	50
Senator 1984-1987	51
Astra MkI 1980-1984	52
Nova 1983-1993	56
The Concept Cars	60
Index	63

Introduction

Following on from the work already done by my co-author, Alan Earnshaw, and I covering the period from 1945 to 1964, it is now my pleasing task to undertake an overview of the next 20-year period. However, when I say overview, I regretfully have to mean just that, because the variety of models produced by Vauxhall in the period 1965 to 1984 was quite considerable. The period saw the small entry-level car change from the HA Viva to the Nova, whilst the larger, more luxurious six-cylinder PC was eventually supplanted by the Senator and Monza Coupé; but this was only after a number of years where there were no six-cylinder cars in the Vauxhall range at all.

In giving this overview it may well be that I have ignored what some readers will consider obvious or essential, but to spread the coverage across the time scale concerned, my approach has had to be subjective. Yet given the superb illustrative material made available to us for this book, I am sure that you will agree that this makes a wonderful record of this period. In the selection of this material I have been greatly assisted by Alan Earnshaw, and (more importantly) the team at Vauxhall Heritage. Most notable in my thanks are Dennis Sherer, Ray Cooper, Dave Hine, Nigel Griggs and Peter Stone at Luton, and Ron Atkins, Peter Blincow and Andrea Wright in Vauxhall Heritage Services.

As space in this volume is so limited, my text presupposes that the reader will have already considered what has been written on the period 1945 to 1964. If not, I would earnestly recommend that this is an essential prerequisite, as this period covers one of the most fascinating eras in the British motor manufacturing industry. The two decades after World War 2 saw such a major change in design, manufacturing and maintenance of British motor vehicles that it almost defies description. Vauxhall was a market leader in that period, with huge sales at home and abroad, yet had come from a virtual standstill on car manufacturing. During the period 1939-1945 the works at Luton were essentially committed to war production, with nearly a quarter of a million trucks, and over 5,000 tanks being produced. Conversely, the number of cars produced in these years barely exceeded three figures!

To illustrate the continuing heritage of Vauxhall, we include in this chapter the three model ranges that were in production at the start of 1965. We begin with the HA, and some lucky person could have won this Deluxe model for the sum of one shilling at this event at Woburn Abbey in August 1965.

Leading us into the era 1965-1984, we show the evolution of the medium-sized Vauxhall, with a line of three Victor models. From left to right we show the FB Super (1964), the FC 101 (1967), and the FD 2000 (1967) in a view taken on the Brache Estate at Luton in August 1967.

Here Britain's 'Steel City' sees the result of its labours as a Firenza Sport 2.3SL is posed for the camera above Sheffield's former Midland Railway station on 19 May 1972. The Firenza was a derivative of the HC Viva range and initially came with a choice of two engine sizes — 1,800cc and two-litre; a third engine size (2.3-litre) was added in 1972.

To go from that standstill to the fantastic car production figures achieved in the 1950s and 1960s was a testament to the drive of the management, and the skill and dedication of the workforce. In 1959 the two-millionth car was produced. It was a time of challenge, innovation, flair and more than a little panache. The panache came with the stylish F-Type Victors and the superb Cresta/Velox PAs, but the one car that swept the board was the new economical HA Viva launched in 1963. It took Britain by storm, and by 1965 a quarter of a million had been built; so it is with this car we begin our story.

Although the HA sold over 300,000 cars, it did not last long into the period covered by this book as it was superseded by the HB Viva in March 1966. Briefly described, the HA Viva saloon was available in three types, the basic, the Deluxe and the SL. The Deluxe was easily identified by the chromium band along the side of the car; the SL had a coloured flash and a more fussy radiator grille. An estate car version was also released in 1964 and went under the name of Bedford Beagle, whilst two car-derived vans, the six-cwt (HAE) and eight-cwt (HAD) were also produced, and a 10cwt version (HAV) appeared in 1973.

The 80mph SL was capable of doing 0 to 50mph in 13sec, due to its 60bhp high compression engine and a Stromberg carburettor; by contrast the basic Viva developed 44bhp at 5,200rpm. The gearbox was a four-speed all-synchromesh unit with a very easy control lever. The top of the range HA90 Viva had front disc brakes, which became optional on all Vivas after 1965. Some 11,794 HA90s were built between 1965 and 1966 when the HA was superseded by the HB model. The Viva had a rather boxy-style with an overall length of 155in (3.9m), and easily accommodated four adults plus a surprising amount of luggage. The price of the base model when new was £436 but with Purchase Tax it came out at £527 7s 11d and found a strong niche among the economy minded car-buying public. Although this was the first small Vauxhall since the 1,203cc Ten-Four of 1937, it proved so popular that with regular updates of styles and performance the Viva remained in production for over 24 years.

The Viva was envisaged as a low-cost economy model aimed at family motoring. Yet, in addition to this market, Vauxhall produced an up-market model, the Viva SL, which is seen here in low autumnal sunlight on 4 October 1965.

Showing the rear-three-quarter aspect of a left-hand drive version of the SL90, we can distinguish the added refinements of the SL (Super Luxury) model. First there is a contrasting side flash, then come white wall tyres and wheel embellishers.

INTRODUCTION

In this rear-three-quarter view of the FC Victor 101 Deluxe, we show the new two-tone paint scheme that looked so impressive on this model. The crisp edges, complete with chrome trim, were a natural dividing point and the roof and boot were painted in a contrasting colour to the basic body shade.

In the FC Victor series, the VX/90 was the top car in the range, and here we see a left-hand drive version of the four-door saloon. It had a 1,594cc engine and produced 81bhp. This gave it a top speed of 90mph, some 10mph more than the basic FC Victor.

Estate versions of the Vauxhall car range had always been popular, although in the early days estate cars were not offered as a factory-built option and this work was passed out to approved bodybuilding firms like Grosvenor, Martin Walter and Friary Motors. With the arrival of the F-Type Victor a factory-built estate was available, and this continued through the Victor era. Here we have a Deluxe FC model, which is finished in two-tone green, in May 1965.

The third Vauxhall model to remain in production at the start of 1965 was the newly introduced PC Cresta. Here we see the estate version of the PC in a view taken in November 1966. However, unlike the Victor, the PC estate was not a factory-built option and approved builders still undertook the conversion work from the saloon car. This one was bodied by the famous Folkestone company of Martin Walter, but production of the estate car version did not last long on the PC and ended early in 1968.

In 1964 Vauxhall announced the replacement for the FB Victor in the shape of the remarkably modern FC, which had much more room inside (thanks to curved side panels and glass) giving more shoulder room. In saloon form, the FC Victor also had a curiously curved rear windscreen. The FC was powered by the enlarged 1,595cc engine (with an increased 69bhp at 4,800rpm), which had appeared in the later FB Victor models. The replacement VX4/90 now produced 81bhp and had a top speed approaching 90mph. Transmission for the FC range was rear-wheel drive through a Borg & Beck eight-inch single dry plate clutch from a three-speed synchromesh gearbox. However four-speed and automatic gearboxes were an optional extra. The chassis was an integral steel

Selling almost one-third of a million models, the HA Viva was undoubtedly the success story of the 1960s. This little Vauxhall took the British market by storm, and this picture is, therefore, very appropriate as this colour is called Storm Grey. The Viva sold very well overseas, and it became a very good export model. Many Vauxhall motorists took their little Viva on to the continent for holidays, and this contrived publicity picture presents the sort of image that captured a new generation of motorists.

structure, having improved suspension with coil springs at the front and semi-elliptic springs at the rear, incorporating Vauxhall telescopic dampers. It had Girling hydraulic brakes with duo servo drums at the rear, but disc brakes were also optional for the front.

The FC range consisted of six models: the Standard saloon, the Super saloon, the Deluxe saloon, the Estate car, the Deluxe Estate and the VX4/90. This range of cars was aimed at the public who wanted a degree of refinement without the extravagance of the top of the range models. Prices went from £678 4s 7d for the Standard saloon, through to £871 11s 3d for the top of the range VX4/90.

Internally the standard saloons had bench seats covered in vinyl, whereas the Deluxe version and VX4/90 had separate front seats. These were also covered in vinyl, but a leather seat trim was an optional extra on the Deluxe models. In the case of the VX4/90, a revised facia panel incorporated gauges for water temperature, amperes and oil pressure in addition to a rev-counter. In the autumn of 1966 a much improved radiator grille appeared on the Standard, Super and Deluxe models, along with small improvements to the trim and changes to the seat design. Improvements to the engine resulted in a rise from 70bhp to 76bhp. The 101 range of cars proved very popular with 219,814 Victors and 13,449 VX4/90s being sold during the production period.

In the new six-cylinder PC models, David Jones and his styling team produced one of the most attractive designs of the era, which even today looks extremely lithe and elegant. It went back to American influence and, although the car's width was reduced by one-inch (25.4mm) over the preceding PB range, the interior dimension was improved thanks again to the use of curved panels and side glass. The overall length was increased by five inches (127mm) and the fuel tank was repositioned resulting in far greater luggage accommodation.

INTRODUCTION

The new PC models, the Cresta and Cresta Deluxe, were powered by the 3,294cc straight-six overhead valve engine that had been introduced on the later PB models in October 1964. This produced 21% more power than the 2.6-litre used in the early PB Velox and Cresta. It now achieved 0 to 50mph in 7.5sec, making it faster than a Porsche 1699SC. Yet the cost was just £807 plus Purchase Tax of £169 13s 9d.

In 1966, the year after the PC was introduced, Vauxhall launched a top of the range flagship model. This was the PC Viscount, which had all the extras of the PC Cresta fitted as standard equipment. As with the Cresta Deluxe, the Viscount used twin headlights but had a new style of radiator grille. An obvious external feature was the fitting of a fabric-covered roof, whilst the Viscount name could be observed in discreet letters on the front wing behind the wheel arch. The Viscount had reclining front seats, a leather trim, walnut veneer, picnic tables, electric windows and reading lights; all the luxury features of a quality car at a premium price. The Powerglide two-speed automatic was standard and a four-speed manual gearbox was available for an £86 reduction in price. In October 1970 a GM three-speed automatic gearbox replaced the two-speed Powerglide. It was immediately reviewed as being a vast improvement over the previous unit. Between 1965 and 1972 no less than 53,912 PC Crestas were produced, whilst figures for the Viscount totalled 7,025 from 1966 to 1972.

At the top end of the Vauxhall range, the PC Cresta launched in 1965 had two models (Deluxe and standard), as the Velox model had been discontinued after the PB production came to an end. To overcome this lack of choice, Vauxhall introduced a new 'flagship' model in 1966. Here we see a PC Viscount, which had a 3.3-litre engine and many 'additional features' as standard.

Model Types

HB Viva 1966-1970

With the introduction of the all-new HB range in March 1966, the Vauxhall Viva-Opel Kadett relationship had something of a role reversal. Whereas the hitherto boxy Viva became much more elegant and fashionable as it employed the 'coke-bottle styling', the Kadett grew more staid and dated-looking.

The new Viva's success was largely due to the styling ability of David Jones' team, who successfully scaled down the design of the PC Cresta for the HB Viva. This design suited the little car extremely well and it proved to be a remarkably profitable model for Vauxhall, as the design in all its 26 variations was enthusiastically received by the motoring public during this period. Three four-cylinder engine sizes covered this range — the 1,159cc, 1,599cc and 1,975cc variants. In addition a Borg Warner automatic transmission was available on all but the basic and the performance versions (but this became an option in 1967).

The 1,159cc engine with four cylinders in line had a bore and stroke of 77.77mm x 61mm, and developed 47bhp at approximately 5,200rpm; breathing was through a Solex PSEI-7 carburettor. Conventional rear-wheel drive was employed using a four-speed all-synchromesh gearbox and a Borg & Beck 6.25in clutch.

The new Viva had an integral steel structure with an independent front suspension system by coil springs and wishbones. It also featured a live rear axle, located by lower trailing arms and diagonal upper arms, and coil springs with Vauxhall telescopic dampers on the rear. At the front it employed Girling disc brakes and had drum brakes at the rear. The maximum speed was an acceptable 80mph and 0-60 was reached in 19.7sec. The fuel consumption was about 30-35mpg. Its economy of purchase and maintenance, related to its performance and handling characteristics, made these models popular in the role of both Police Panda cars and mini-cabs (and a lot of other things in between).

An improved performance model was launched in the guise of the HB90, and this used a Stromberg carburettor instead of a Solex model. The HB90s were good for 85mph and, like the Deluxe and the SLs, were available with automatic transmission. The 90

Opposite top: From a picture taken for the 1968/69 General Motors' Annual Report, we see a view of a four-door HB Viva taken on 14 November 1968. The fashionable design of the HB is clearly shown in this view, which makes quite a contrast from even the most luxurious HA Viva SLs.

Opposite bottom: Here we show one of the pre-production models of the HB Viva SLs in a view that was taken in May 1966. This model carries the plain radiator grille of three horizontal strips, whereas the picture above shows the centrally divided grille made up from eight horizontal chrome strips. The really interesting feature about this picture is the fact that the car carries white wall tyres, a feature that the authors have never seen on any other HB Viva.

Showing the rear aspect of a pair of HB Vivas, with an SL model (JHV 826D) and a 1200 saloon (JHV 795D) on the Vauxhall Test Track at Chaul End. In addition to the SL badge on the boot of the former, the other identifying feature of the SL is the chrome strip running along the boot edge and round the rear light clusters.

and SL were easily distinguished by the three-bar radiator grille whereas the basic, the Brabham and the 1600 all had a radiator grille of fine bars with a central vertical division. The well-respected coach-building firm of Crayford also offered a convertible version of the two-door SL and the SL90 HB Viva. These were extremely stylish and almost European looking cars, but survivors are now extremely rare.

The standard HB Viva was such a popular car during its production that it was often the subject of the glamorous top prize in various television game shows and competitions. It also achieved considerable fame as a fleet car and companies like Stork Margarine, McDougall's Flour, Radio Rentals, Granada and Fine Fare Supermarkets used them to promote their products or services. In such instances the car was appropriately sign-written to represent the company in question, and usually accompanied by female representatives dressed in promotional uniforms! The cars then often wound up outside supermarkets, in shopping centres or other places where the public were present in large numbers. As a result, the new HB Viva featured in many television commercials and Vauxhall got much welcomed publicity as a result.

The HB Viva was not only a model for show; it was also a car with plenty of go in it. It was extensively raced and rallied during its career by such high profile drivers as Des Donnelly, Jim Thompson, Bill Dryden and, of course, Gerry Marshall.

Willem Blydenstein, who successfully raced a number of cars in the 1960s, including Minis, not only drove but also tuned his cars. This talented individual (from Dutch and Norwegian parents) then campaigned with VX4/90s. He also became heavily involved in tuning and racing Vauxhalls and, with 130 outright wins and 20 international rally

MODEL TYPES

wins, his name became synonymous with high performance Vauxhalls. In 1970 Blydenstein had the task of returning Vauxhall to international competition after a long absence and what a return it was; during 1971 Vivas won all the major saloon championships, including the Irish and Scottish saloon car championships, the BARC hill climb and the Osram/GEC special saloon car championship.

Right: In 1969 eight new four-door saloons were added to the Viva range, bringing the number of available variations up to 26. Here we have a four-door 1600 Deluxe model fitted with the 1,599cc ohc engine. The pre-publicity picture was taken in the autumn of 1968.

Below: Looking now at variations of the HB saloon, we first of all consider the estate, and to do this illustrate the top of the range SL model. This was an attractive and stylish two-door model, which boasted a long, sleek side window. What is not that well known is the fact that Vauxhall also produced a few of these vehicles as a two-seater light commercial, with a steel panel replacing the glass window. Yet this van was never really developed and the HA-based light commercials remained in production until 1985.

Vauxhall Cars 1965-1984

A complete contrast to all the rest of the HB range was the Crayford conversion that formed one of the most attractive convertible (cabriolet) cars of the era. From a first glance you would not think that this was a Vauxhall for, by losing its hard top, the SL90 takes on an appearance of something like the Triumph Stag. Note the bumper over-riders, chrome tail-pipe and covered spot lamps among the many added extras. The sole dealer for this model was Wallace Arnold of Leeds, and survivors of the convertible are about as rare as hen's teeth!

In 1966 and 1967 the driver Jack Brabham took the World Constructor's Championships in the Australian-developed Repco Formula One car. Its engine had its origins in the American Buick V8, which was also a GM product, so it was not unnatural for the relationship to develop between Brabham and Vauxhall Motors. The Brabham Viva that resulted was never really a racing car, but it did carry the FIA Group 2 racing certification. In many ways it was an image car with a sporty look, enjoying a marked improvement in acceleration and the ability to rev to 7,000rpm without undue stress.

MODEL TYPES

The engine of the Brabham Viva is shown in this picture, and the modifications are clearly seen. Most obvious are the aluminium manifolds leading to the side-draught twin-carbs and the Brabham name. There was also a high-lift camshaft and a new exhaust system.

The year 1967 was very important to Vauxhall in general, and the HB Viva in particular. This was the year that the HB became available in estate car form, but in reality this development was the period equivalent to the modern-day hatchback. Also launched that year was the Jack Brabham engine conversion, which was available on the SL models. In this modified power unit, the 1,159cc Viva engine had been tuned to produce 79bhp with a new cylinder head. It also utilised twin carbs and a new manifold. The Brabham Viva had distinctive bonnet flashes of a contrasting colour, but was only produced from 1967 to 1968 as it was superseded by a new Viva model called the GT.

Another 1967 event that should also be recorded is the company's increasing commitment to safety and customer satisfaction. This was noted even in small cars like the HB Viva, which would later benefit from the introduction of a collapsible steering column.

By the middle of 1968, the HB Viva export market had substantially increased, and during the period from January to July 44% more Vivas were exported when compared to the comparable period in 1967. The months of January to July were traditionally a period when efforts were concentrated on export sales, as (from 1967) the registration letter changed on 1 August annually, making the period from then to December a busy time for sales in the home market.

In June 1968 the range expanded still further with the addition of two new four-door saloons and a three-door estate, in Deluxe and SL trim. Also in 1968, a 1,600cc Viva was introduced; this used the 83bhp 1.6-litre cogged-belt ohc engine from the FD Victor. The GT version of the HB was also deliberately conceived as a performance car, and this model was achieved by slipping the two-litre engine from the Vauxhall FD Victor into the Viva's shell. All the early GT Vivas had matt-black bonnets, but this feature was deleted in 1969, although the Viva GT remained in production until 1970.

Other models in the Viva HB range included the aforementioned three-door estate car, which was introduced in June 1967. This stylish estate could accommodate loads up to five feet (1.52m) in length with the rear passenger seats folded down. They also made a modestly successful emergency ambulance, and one of these (an ex-North Riding of Yorkshire ambulance), was well used as a personnel carrier/first aid post by a mountain rescue team in the Pennines until the early 1980s.

The basic Viva HB saw 566,901 units produced between 1966 and 1970. The HB 90 achieved 78,296, the HB 1600 13,517, while the Viva GT saw 4,606 units produced from 1968 until 1970. The cost of the HB in 1966 was £626 2s 9d (including Purchase Tax of £118 2s 9d) — a very reasonable sum for such a lively, modern car.

15

After its great racing successes in the early years, Vauxhall ignored the sport in the post-World War 2 era. There were sponsor deals, and the marque featured in many rallies — including the Monte Carlo. However, it fell to a dealer-led initiative to get things moving again, and with this came a degree of success as the Vauxhall name reappeared on the saloon car circuit. In this 1971 picture we show the famous quartet of 'Vauxhall' drivers of the early 1970s with, from left to right, Des Donelly (Irish Saloon Car Champion), Jim Thompson (Scottish Saloon Car Champion), Bill Dryden (BARC Hill-Climb Champion) and Gerry Marshall, who had just won the first Osram Saloon Car Championship. Along with their Viva GT cars, the drivers celebrate their respective successes at Ellesmere Port.

The late-1960s was the era of the HB Viva and the 'Spaghetti Western', here a HB Viva Estate is pictured in Spain at one of the filming locations. And, for a fist full of dollars...

'This year we're off to sunny Spain', sang pop-star Sylvia, but in Vauxhall's case it wasn't Viva Espania, it was Victor Great Britain. In the superbly sunny Spanish setting, such a contrast from Luton in November, we see a 1967 publicity shot of a Victor 2000. Finished in a pale blue monotone scheme, the FD Victor might not have had the panache of the earlier two-tone Victor models, but it certainly had superb styling lines.

FD Victor 1967-1972

In 1967, the company that had been formed as the Vauxhall Iron Works was now a hundred years old and, with much celebration, the launch of its new models reflected this fact. One of these was the FD Victor, with its ultra trans-Atlantic styling, which superseded the FC101 Victor. This styling was crisp, sharp and up to date. It also had a notable waist crease to break down the slab-sided effect, rather than using a chrome band. This, along with the raise in the panel work of the rear doors, emphasised the length of the car. With its nicely raked front and rear screens, these models harmonised with the PC and HB models that had been introduced in 1965 and 1966 respectively.

Initially the FD range was available as the 1600 or 2000 Victor using a new hemispherical head, belt-driven overhead cam four-cylinder engine of 1,599cc and 1,975cc respectively. Steering was now by rack-and-pinion, front discs were optional on the 1600, and a three-speed column gear change was standard; but four on the floor was optional (with or without overdrive). This was virtually the same gearbox as had been used in the previous FC 101 Victor.

An early FD Victor (probably another two-litre model) is being taken along the paved road at Chaul End Testing Ground. This left-hand drive model was just one of a number of cars that underwent extensive testing before the model was launched — other tests included extreme arctic weather conditions in Scandinavia.

In 1967 the new Victor was awarded the Don Safety Trophy, as the vehicle making the greatest contribution to road safety that year. Here we have a picture of an export model seen at the Helsingør Shipyards in Denmark during the summer of 1968.

This view shows the rear-three-quarter view of the two-litre FD Victor, along with a then novel feature — reversing lights.

Estate cars were introduced in May 1968 and the Strasbourg automatic gearbox was available from October 1969, at which time the models were renamed Victor Super. The estate car could accommodate 60.5cu ft of luggage, and like the saloon counterpart it featured a collapsible steering column. This was due to Vauxhall's continuing commitment to safety and, as a result, the Victor 2000 was awarded the Don Safety Trophy.

Some suspension features were shared with the Viva, such as the rubber-mounted sub-frame for the front suspension. But at the back, there were five suspension points in the

Another 1968 picture, this time presenting the 1,600cc FDW Victor; the 'W' represented the code for an estate car version. Factory-built, these stylish estate cars were considerably ahead of their time, and would be eventually emulated by the MkIII Ford Cortina Estate, which carried a similar body style when viewed from the side.

form of parallel trailing arms plus a Panhard rod, instead of the Viva's four inclined links.

In October 1969 a new performance version of the Vauxhall Victor was announced. This was the VX4/90, sharing the same body shell as the FD Victor, but while the Victor had a fine mesh grille, the VX4/90 had a black radiator grille, highlighted by a white cross, but still using dual headlights. Also, externally fitted to the VX4/90 were Rostyle wheels, long before these became a popular accessory. Also evident were the coachlines emphasising the car's 'coke-bottle styling' and rear-wing stone guards.

With its introduction, a performance model was back in the Vauxhall line-up after an absence of two years. The new VX4/90 used twin carburettors and overdrive as part of the standard package. It employed the 1,975cc engine, with four-cylinders in-line that had a bore and stroke of 96.25mm x 69.24mm. This developed 112bhp at 5,400rpm and utilised the Zenith 175CD-25 variable choke carburettors. Transmission was by a four-speed all-synchromesh gearbox through a Borg & Beck eight-inch diaphragm spring clutch, although Laycock de Normanville overdrive was available as an optional extra.

Still designated VX4/90, the '4' remained appropriate as it still had four cylinders, but the '90' was rather inappropriate as the top speed was 101mph. The VX4/90 remained in production until January 1972. Production figures reached 14,271, the price was £970 plus £283 8s 1d Purchase Tax, giving a total cost of £1,253 8s 1d in 1970.

The other models to share the FD body shell were the Ventora and the Victor 3300, both of which were introduced in 1968. These models came about by fitting the FD body shell with the 3.3-litre six-cylinder engine from the PC range of Vauxhalls. Although this Chevrolet

Even from the front view, there was a vague familiarity with the MkIII Cortina, which many considered to be 'the estate car' for the early 1970s. Yet, at the time that Vauxhall introduced the Victor in 1967, its 'coke-bottle' styling was way ahead of its time. The design, said to be influenced from a famous American soft-drink bottle laid on its side, was even more suited to the estate, introduced in 1968. Here we see a 1969 two-litre version on the Brache Estate opposite the Luton works.

designed engine had been introduced in the 1950s, it still proved to be reasonably trouble free and despite the performance only being on par with the VX4/90's engine, this was a smooth and quiet unit. The name given to the estate car was the Victor 3300, but it shared the same 'egg crate' radiator grille of the Ventora saloon. From 1970 until 1972 the slightly improved Ventora was renamed the Ventora II and the 3300 estate became the Ventora. Production figures for the Ventora reached 25,185. The purchase price was £1,101 16s 6d, but extras cost £9 10s for a vinyl roof, the radio was £27 16s, fog and spot lights £11 2s 6d, reversing lights £3 14s 6d, wing mirrors £3 19s and the cigar lighter was £1 12s.

With almost half a million FD models being produced (including the Ventora), it is not surprising that they became a common sight on Britain's roads, and it very squarely captured a sector of the market where other British manufacturers were in decline. This is, therefore, probably an opportune time in this narrative to break off and look at what Vauxhall's main competitors were offering. Austin, now part of BMC, had its 1,795cc ohv 1800 model, of which 210,000 were built between 1964 and 1975, and it also launched a three-litre version in 1967.

At the top end of the FD estate range came the superbly appointed Victor 3.3, which along with the Ventora effectively superseded the last of the PCs. The problem with fitting the 3.3 six-cylinder engine into the Victor bonnet was one of space, and it must also be borne in mind that this actual engine dated back to the 1950s and was quite dated when compared to the four-cylinder unit normally fitted in the 1600 and two-litre FD models.

MODEL TYPES

In this view of another 3.3 estate dating from November 1967, we see a pre-production model on a publicity photo-shoot. It represented the ultimate Vauxhall car of the period, but a new model (the Ventora) was destined to become the top of the range in 1970.

Left: Following the Victor by a full six months, and employing a 3,294cc engine of Chevrolet origin, this stylish saloon became the top of the range. It carried a full range of luxury appointments, including an array of instrumentation set in a neat facia panel. A few of these early Ventoras had a rosewood finish to the interior (door trim, dash, etc) and this became standard on the Ventora II models. A feature of the early Ventora models, like the top of the range PCs, was the fitting of the Powerglide Automatic Transmission system. This was later superseded by the GM Strasbourg transmission on the Ventora II.

Ford had the successful MkIV Zephyr/Zodiac models on the go, and these were really the FD's main competitors. In all some 149,263 of these cars would be produced by Vauxhall's great rivals between 1966 and 1971, but this is nearly 50,000 less than the FD figures for the period from 1967 to 1972, Ford enthusiasts might claim that this figure was affected by sales of the top of the range MkII 1.6 Cortinas, but neither of these Dagenham offerings had quite the flair of the Vauxhall car, and it showed.

Near rivals Hillman had its superb 1,725cc Hunter models, which ran in production from 1966 to 1977 and witnessed a build total of almost half a million, but at £989 it was considerably dearer than the basic FD. Rootes, the owners of Hillman, was undergoing major changes internally for, in 1967, the controlling financial interests had been acquired by another of GM's archrivals, Chrysler. A 13% holding was retained by the British government, but massive changes were to follow. Another possible merger — this time between BMC and Leyland — first came to light in 1967, but the main rival to the FD from BMC, the 1,622cc Morris Oxford, was already a dated (albeit frequently revised) design that had appeared in its first form in 1959.

Triumph on the other hand had its superb 2.0 six-in-line saloon cum sports car, which had a build figure of 120,645 between 1963 and 1969. In 1968 Triumph introduced its 2.5PI version and, although only nine thousand or so were built up to 1969, it quickly found success in a market where the Victor range had traditionally enjoyed good sales. This was the police authority market, and in almost every way (except price) the FD was beaten hands down by the top flight Triumph. Yet with a £350 difference in the price, many Watch Committees or Chief Constables were reluctant to change from the Vauxhalls they had loved and trusted since the end of World War 2. Mind you, in the general market the competition then coming from foreign markets was not such an easy thing to combat; in particular the Swedish Volvo 123 and 140 series presented a serious threat by the end of the decade.

That said, the FD still had a major share of the market, and it was a good-looking, comfortable car for its price, but if only the build quality had lived up to the mechanical standards. Sadly the quality of steel being used in the body shell tended to deteriorate in adverse conditions, thus echoing a problem that had dogged other Vauxhall models in the past. I suspect, that having heavily invested in a superb paint plant and anti-corrosion system, Vauxhall tended to rely a bit too heavily on it.

Even so, there was another big threat facing the FD Victor, and all the other big cars being produced at that time, the spectre of high taxes. For a start, Purchase Tax on cars went up to 36.6% in November 1968, whilst petrol had reached the astronomical sum of six shillings per gallon. Added to this there was another major blow to sales of the bigger Vauxhalls, as the Labour government (trying to damp down the economy) made the minimum Hire Purchase deposit for car purchase a massive 40% and cut the maximum repayment period to just two years. Yet the road spending programme, instituted by a Conservative government a decade earlier showed no signs of slowing down, and by 1971 the UK had 1,000 miles of motorway for the FDs to travel on.

The other luxury car in the FD range was the VX4/90, which was introduced at the Paris Motor Show in October 1969 and seen here in this rear three-quarter view on 12 August 1971.

In the most idyllic of settings we have the four-door HC Viva SL. As the car features a vinyl roof covering, it is probably the 1.6- or two-litre version. To emphasise the 'life-style' enjoyed by owners of such a luxurious family saloon, the photographer has posed a 'hunting, shooting and fishing' type character in the background complete with his spaniel and a brace of 'bagged' pheasants.

HC VIVA 1970-1979

With the increasing pressures of the British economy of the late 1960s impacting heavily on sales of the bigger models from the car manufacturing industry, a glut of small- to mid-range cars began to appear in the early 1970s. The biggest success of all was the MkIII Cortina from Ford, of which 1,126,559 were produced between 1970 and 1976. Less successful was the roomy, but bulky-looking BMC Maxi, which was revamped and given a new gearbox. The launch of the all-new Hillman Avenger — with a choice of 1,248cc or 1,498cc engines — was also to have a major impact on the market in which the Viva was aimed. So too was the new Triumph 1500, which replaced the earlier 1300/1300TC models.

It was, therefore, something of a crowded field into which Vauxhall launched the final version of the Viva in October 1970. This followed on the alphabetical sequence and became the HC, which was to remain in production for nine years. This new design was two inches (50.8mm) wider and one inch (25.4mm) longer than the HB. This neat and tidy little car benefited from a greater glass area than that used in the HB, but at the same time it lost the 'coke-bottle' style and thereby gained the appearance of a rather higher car.

The new Viva was launched at the Paris Motor Show and, like its predecessor, it became an instant success. Four engine sizes were offered, but one of these, the 1,159cc — which was carried over from the HB range — was replaced in August 1971 by a larger 1,256cc overhead valve unit (which, in turn, was later used in the Chevette).

Other engine sizes were the 1,599cc (which was replaced in 1972 by the larger 1,759cc) and the 110bhp 2,279cc engine. These two larger engine models later would later become the Magnum saloon and estate when the HC range was substantially revised in 1973.

At the other end of the scale, the basic 1200 model did not command nearly so much attention for its photo-shoot. Nevertheless, this model sold exceptionally well in both two- and four-door versions, and had an obvious appeal to the economy-minded motorist of the early 1970s.

To illustrate the rear aspect of the Vauxhall Viva HC saloon, we chose this view of yet another 1200 model. From this it will be seen that the 'coke-bottle styling' of the earlier HB has now been firmly left behind in an attempt to create an entirely new style for the 1970s.

The new HC Viva was available in four body styles: a two-door saloon, a four-door saloon, a three-door estate and an attractive coupé. It had three levels of trim option available: Standard, Deluxe and SL. The styling of the estate foreshadowed the fastback style of the FE estate, which would supersede the FD range in 1972. As stated, these styling changes brought about a greater area of side glass than on the previous HB Vivas, but owing to the fastback style of the estate car, luggage accommodation was greatly affected.

The year after the introduction of the HC Viva, Luton made use of HC technology and components to produce a new 'sports' model, the stylish Vauxhall Firenza. We will deal with this later, but it was closely related to the Viva. In fact the remnants of the Firenza body shell stock were later used in the Viva E, which was marketed as an economy coupé.

On 20 July 1971, Luton works achieved the distinction of building its 1,000,000th Viva, whilst chassis number 1,000,001 was produced at Vauxhall's Ellesmere Port plant. By 1973 the overhead camshaft Vivas were being tested at the new 700-acre Millbrook facility with its huge two-mile motorway standard speed saucer and 1.5 miles of country roads. Improvements for the 1974 line up of HC Vivas included the SL model, with wider wheels and fashionable matt black (non-reflective) wiper blades and arms.

Although Vauxhall sold only half as many HC Vivas as Ford sold MkIII Cortinas, the overall build figure was still a staggering 640,863 cars. Yet there is no apparent explanation as to why the HC did not go on to achieve even greater things. For example, with an introductory price of £783, the base line HC Viva was £131 cheaper than the basic 1.3 MkIII Cortina. The costliest Cortina, the top of the line estate, cost £1,732 whereas the HC SL estate was just £1,055, so there must have been something else.

Above: In contrast to the basic models shown on page 24, we have a view of the limited edition two-litre SL. The Gold Ribbon HC Viva featured many additional extras as standard fittings, including the Rostyle alloy wheels clearly seen in this view taken near the Luton works in autumn 1971.

Right: At the upper end of the scale, we have the 2300 HP 'Droopsnoot' estate. Typical of the period it came with sporty wheels and obligatory 'go-faster' stripes along the side.

Right: Like the earlier Vivas, an estate version of the HC was to prove popular with buyers at home and abroad, and once again the two-door format was adopted. However, the rear door was much more like a hatch than the previous tailgates on the Viva HB and the load space appeared to be (but actually was not) substantially less than the HB model. That does not seem to distract this young lady, wearing the height of 1970s fashion, as she loads up her 1600 estate at a market garden in July 1971.

OK, if you thought that the high-performance estate had 'go-faster' stripes along the side — what about this 2.3-litre estate. Bearing the legend Viva Ecosse Equip on the rear flanks, this 1973 'sports' edition was supplied by the famous Scottish Vauxhall dealers, SMT, and is pictured near the Forth railway bridge north of Edinburgh.

A study of comparisons in the car magazines of the period do not reveal anything exceptional, except that the HC seemed a bit 'tinny' to one reviewer, to another 'the gear stick lacked the smooth flow of the Ford transmission'. But in all other respects what Vauxhall scored in one department, Ford lost and vice-versa. Perhaps it all boiled down to style, and my co-author Alan and my brother Michael both ran MkIII Cortinas, Alan had a two-litre GLX estate, and Michael a 1.6 XL saloon. There was something of a social standing about being a Cortina owner in the early 1970s, and it was apparent that many people, who were given the choice of a company car, were purchasing the Ford offering.

That is not to say the Viva HC did not have its adherents, and there were several large firms who ran quite large fleets in my hometown of Huddersfield; David Brown Gears had them, whilst its counterpart David Brown Tractors conversely ran Hillman Avengers. ICI had another HC fleet and it seems to be a factor that the bigger the fleet, the more likely it was that the Viva would be purchased. Cumulative costs must have played a large part in this equation, but in general terms, for every HC that was sold, two Cortinas would hit the streets.

This takes nothing away from the HC, and it spanned a decade in which Glam Rock, hot pants and Skinheads came and went. By the end though, and despite a number of facelifts the Viva was looking a bit dated. It was never really replaced as such, but many of its loyal adherents went on to become purchasers of the Cavalier, which had made its first appearance in 1975 as we will discuss later.

The HC Viva three-door estate (super hatchback) model.

26

Now for the ultimate in body styles (and obviously I mean the car), we have another really stunning publicity picture from the early-1970s. Seen here on 5 May 1972, is the Firenza Coupé. This is actually a GT version, as can be determined by the round twin headlamps, as those on the Deluxe were square ones.

FIRENZA 1971-1973

A very close development of the HC Vauxhall Viva came in 1971 when a modified body shell was produced under the name Vauxhall Firenza. This new coupé was obviously planned to appeal to the buyers of the Ford Capri, but despite the body shell's appearance in several guises the project was neither as successful as Vauxhall had hoped nor as the model deserved to be.

The graceful lines of the Firenza were first brought to the public's attention a year after the HC Viva had made its debut. The Firenza had the same 97in (246cm) wheelbase as the saloon model and at first it was offered with the same 1,159cc engine as the Viva. However, in 1972 this 62bhp ohv power unit was increased in size to 1,256cc for, although being smooth and quiet, it was heavily criticised for being slow and feeble.

The extra power was really needed because, contrary to the illusion that the coupé was a lithe creature, it had increased 65lb (29.5k) in weight over the saloon thus making the Firenza Coupé a sort of sheep in wolf's clothing. Before long the 1,600cc ohc engine was offered as an alternative. Also available was the 2000SL, which was capable of 100mph.

Better performance Firenzas were offered in the guise of the 1800 and 2300 GT ohc models, which were easily identified by their twin round headlights. It was these two models that went on for further development in 1973 when they reappeared as the Magnum Coupé that remained in production until 1977. Vauxhall also offered the Viva E Coupé, an economy model to use up the remaining stocks of the Firenza and Magnum coupé body shells. This economy model was powered by the 1,256cc engine and, when introduced in 1975, it cost just £1,399. The total production figure for the Firenza was 18,352.

The body styling of the HC Firenza can clearly be seen in this picture of a Viva E. The style may well have been a unique coupé in the Vauxhall range, but many commentators at the time thought that it was very much a copy of the Ford Capri and in other ways it was critically reviewed as well.

With the Firenza getting a rather unfair press (which it really did not deserve), sales did not meet expectations. To soak up the number of body shells that had already been produced, the HC Viva E was built, but this used the standard 1,256cc engine. The E in the designation stood for Economy, but nevertheless it provided a popular little sports coupé model for 'would-be sports car drivers' at a very modest price.

In this series of three pictures, all featuring the same car (VXD 594M), we see the various aspects of the unique styling on the High Performance Firenza 'Droopsnoot'. Taking the air-dam front end concept of the newly designed (but yet to be introduced) Cavalier and Chevette into public view for the first time, the glass-fibre front end of the car is clearly demonstrated. In these views, showing front, rear and side elevations, the clean crisp lines of the sporting coupé are clearly appreciated. What a pity that only some 200 of these innovatively-designed cars were ever produced.

Firenza 'Droopsnoot' 1973-1975

As stated earlier, Vauxhall's new 'sports' body style was to give Vauxhall a foothold in what had become the rather lucrative market of personalised transport. This was a market almost totally dominated by the Ford Capri, but in theory the Firenza, with its rather stylish body shape, should have been an admirable contender. It offered far more luggage space, but the rear seat was a little cramped for two adults.

Yet the critics panned the model on introduction, giving the 1,256cc engine a very hard review. Not deterred, Vauxhall reduced the number of Firenza models to two and rebranded the larger models, which were launched at the 1972 Motor Show. The first of these was officially called the Vauxhall Firenza HP Coupé, but it immediately gained the unofficial title 'Droopsnoot', on account of the innovative front end. This was a glassfibre panel that was angled from the leading edge of the bonnet to the bumper, incorporating a full width air intake and a spoiler below the bumper. In its styling this was one of the most exciting new cars for years, and it had the performance to match. The engine used in the production cars was the four-cylinder 2,279cc, but it had been given a modified cylinder head, twin Stromberg 175CD-2SE carburettors and a special exhaust manifold, which developed 131bhp at 5,500rpm. It had rear-wheel drive and transmission was through an all-synchromesh ZF five-speed gearbox and a Borg & Beck clutch.

It was a very smart looking car with a really distinctive finish, having Silver Starfire metallic paintwork, matt black window surrounds, and stylish alloy wheels. But the real problem for Vauxhall's entry in to this market was the fact that the Capri was already very well established, and Ford had more or less got everything right. It stood to reason that such a new market would be difficult to enter, but this was compounded by the fact that Vauxhall had concentrated on family saloons for such a long while; indeed the only offerings of a sporting nature from Luton had been the VX4/90s and the Brabham HB Viva.

With the 'Droopsnoot', Vauxhall was hoping for the more exclusive end of the performance/image car market and had hopes for a long production life. In 1974 an estate version based on the Magnum estate — but sharing the same nose cone as the HP coupé — was also offered. Sadly the Firenza was born during a period in British history when industrial unrest, strikes, material shortages and even a three-day working week were the norm. In the end a mere 204 coupés were produced, and this has made the high performance Firenza a highly collectable classic and a real 'cult' car.

MAGNUM 1973-1977

In the 1973 revision of the HC range, a decision was taken to only keep the Viva name on those models with the 1,256cc four-cylinder engines, in the two- or four-door saloon, the estate and the Viva E coupé forms. The models with the 1.8 and the 2.3-litre engines went up market and gained the name Magnum, perhaps merely as a new marketing ploy for the 1970s. This new name had a much more positive and decisive ring to it and, whereas the name Viva suggested gaiety and merriment, Magnum spoke of ability and performance.

With the new name came a new image. The Magnum had four headlamps set in a new matt black radiator grille, which also had a very discreet chrome surround. The grille still retained a central division. A thin rubbing strip appeared along the car's sides, whilst the chrome bumpers now had a black rubber insert. Rostyle wheels with radial ply tyres were now a standard fitment on the entire range. Interiors were redesigned and given reclining seats as well as an improved facia panel.

When the Firenza range was cut back to just two models in 1973, the two larger HCs became the Magnum. This involved the HC models with engine sizes of 1,759cc and 2,279cc. Three body styles were available: saloon, estate and coupé. Here we have a two-door 1800 model (1,769cc) pictured just before the rebranding took place in 1973.

Above: This was the 1800 estate car version, which Vauxhall said 'combines the luxury specification and lively performance of the new Magnum range with 51.5cu ft of usable load space.' The wing mirrors were an optional extra, as were the special wheels. This picture dates from March 1973, but was not approved for release until 21 September 1973.

And, talking about the luxury of the interior, here it is. This represents the only version of the 2.3 Coupé model that we have thus far found in the official records, but it does illustrate the range and clearly shows the appointments a Vauxhall driver could expect in the early 1970s.

According to the 1974 brochure, the Magnum range consisted of the 1,800cc two-door saloon that sold for £1,304, whilst the four-door saloon cost £42 more! The 2.3-litre as a two-door saloon cost £1,409, and the four-door model cost £41 more. Also available were the estate car models but, although considered very stylish, they continued to attract criticism due to their inability to accommodate bulky square loads because of their almost coupé-style tailgates; the 1.8- and 2.3-litre estate cars sold for £1,424 and £1,528 respectively. The final model on offer was the Magnum coupé with either 1,800 or 2,300cc engine size priced at £1,359 and £1,464. The Magnum range was to remain in production until 1977, although the Viva models continued to be produced until 1979.

Starting at the top end of the range, for a change, we begin this selection of FE Victor pictures with a view of the 1976 VX2300. This view, taken on 12 December 1975, shows the car that Vauxhall was planning to take over from the six-cylinder Ventora, which was due to be discontinued in 1976. The road to the development of the VX2300 had begun with special 2.3-litre editions of the FD back in 1974, and the market proved responsive to the further development of a 'top flight' and very powerful four-cylinder car. The VX2300 had moulded seats upholstered in Ambla, whilst the Ventora models had a rather attractive rosewood facia trim. Other improvements, made to increase shoulder room and rear legroom, were all part of Vauxhall's commitment to customer satisfaction.

FE Victor, VX1800 and VX2300 1972-1978

The final Vauxhall cars to carry the Victor, VX/490 and Ventora badges were introduced during February 1972. The FE models utilised a very similar design as the FD models, but they now had a much more upright look along with a larger area of glass than before. Furthermore, in what was reputed to be David Jones' last styling exercise before he retired, the traditional Vauxhall flutes had returned to grace the bonnets of these cars.

The model range now consisted of the Victor, Victor SL, Victor Estate, VX4/90, and the Ventora. Each model employed a deep radiator grille that was dissected by a simple chrome bumper, but those on the Victors were thin horizontal bars with a broad central vertical division, whilst the VX4/90 grille had a more boxy style in black, which was easily recognised by a white cross.

All FEs were built on the same 105in (2.67m) wheelbase, which had increased from 102in (2.59m) on the FD models. This was due to the fact that the FEs carried more weight. For the same reason the engine size went up to 1,800cc, and this was achieved by increasing the cylinder bore to 95.25mm from the FDs 85.73mm, but the stroke remained the same at 69.24mm.

The larger engine was also increased in bore size from 85.73mm to 97.54mm, but the stroke on this engine remained at 76.20mm; it then developed 2,279cc.

Slightly lower in the pecking order, but still a high-class saloon, came the VX1800. Slightly underpowered for its body shell (plus extra appointments), the wise money was spent on the VX2300 if you wanted that bit of extra performance. In relation to the extra cost of £117 between the two cars, the choice was almost obvious.

From the driving seat of the Victor, the road ahead was viewed over a steering wheel with a broad horizontal padded bar, whilst the steering wheel of the sporting VX4/90 had a traditional three-spoke wheel with a central boss. Features on the facia were also different, for on the driver's left above the heater controls the VX4/90 had gauges for the battery condition meter and oil pressure gauge. A switch to the left of the heater controls was used to control the luxury of a heated rear window.

The Victor models had two main gauges, which were the speedometer on the right and a combined petrol/temperature gauge with ignition and oil warning lights on the left. However, on the VX/490 the left hand aperture was taken up by a tachometer with ignition and oil warning lights; the petrol and temperature gauges were therefore in the position occupied by the choke control and manual windscreen washer switches on the Victor. The bonnet release knob and the combined headlamp beam/flasher, indicator and horn switch were the same on both models falling readily at hand on the driver's right.

The basic FE models started with the new 1800cc engine with a four-speed gearbox as standard, although the GM automatic gearbox was an optional extra. Also available were the SL saloon and estate models, but these were fitted with the 2,300cc engine, as was the VX4/90. However, the VX4/90 also had twin carburettors and a four-speed gearbox with overdrive as standard, but was also available with an automatic version.

The Victor models had single high-watt headlamps with the sidelights and indicators located to the side (in the same housing). Conversely, the VX4/90 and the six-cylinder Ventora used dual headlamps of a square style, which were designed to harmonise with the radiator style. On these models the sidelights and indicators were set below the headlamps and just beneath the radiator grille.

33

Vauxhall Cars 1965-1984

I recall that my brother-in-law bought a VX2300 estate version, when purchasing a three-year-old FE in the early 1980s. However, at the age of just six it was scrapped due to corrosion problems, so we took out the engine and sold it for further service in a Bedford CF van. Mechanically the engine was superb, but on that particular car, the body did not last nearly long enough. Here we have an 1800 version pictured on the Brache Estate at Luton.

Although the FE range of Vauxhall models was discontinued in February 1976 after four years production, this was not the last of them. March that year saw the delivery of the VX model range to the Vauxhall dealerships and these were, in effect, the FE Vauxhalls with modified engines, gearboxes and rear axles.

The 'new' VX1800 and VX2300 models appeared in 1976, following the advent of the Cavalier, which effectively superseded the Victor. The Cavalier was basically designed to target the same market as the Ford Cortina and the British Leyland Marina, a role which it really did well. But rather than discontinue the successful body shell of the FE, it was decided to move it up-market for a short while to soak up remaining component stocks.

Both saloon and estate car versions were offered, but as the six-cylinder Ventora had also been discontinued, one of these new VX models had to assume Vauxhall's executive mantle until the Opel Senator (then under development in Germany) was ready for the British market. So Vauxhall's top car became the VX2300 GLS, which outwardly used a radiator grille similar to the Ventora and was offered in a selection of new paint colours that harmonised with the vinyl roof covering. To add style, a discreet chrome trim was fitted to the wheel arches and the door sills. A spoiler was fitted at the front, whilst power steering and a tachometer (as fitted to the VX4/90) were among the other appointments.

A Vauxhall designation that had long signified four-cylinder 90mph, the VX4/90, was a bit inaccurate by the time the FE VX4/90s came along. The basic 1800 was actually capable of achieving just over this figure (91.7mph) whilst the VX2300 could manage over a ton (101.2mph). In some ways this was an odd situation, because whilst some motor manufacturers were actually overstating the performance of their models, Vauxhall was understating the performance in sticking with the VX4/90 badge. Maybe it was a case of sticking with a familiar name that the public could identify with!

MODEL TYPES

The last of the FE models was the Ventora, which was effectively replaced in January 1976 by the VX2300 GLS. The car in this picture is, therefore, the last major up-date to the Ventora marque (which spanned back to 1968), as the model changes thereafter were largely cosmetic. Seen in Hertfordshire in September 1972, this car was to be used for publicity purposes in the 1973 brochures.

The VX4/90 was also given a facelift for this range. This gave a car with a new headlamp style, matt-black side window frames, a front spoiler and Rostyle wheels. When these VX models were introduced in 1976 the price was £2,709 for the saloon and £2,920 for the estate cars, which was really over-priced for what they were. Surprisingly 25,185 were produced. The VX range of models was not intended to have a long production run and they were withdrawn in 1978.

Originally known as the 3300 estate car, styling changes coincided with a name change to the 3.3-litre Ventora Estate in October 1973. This new 1974 model, shown here in a picture from August 1973, still featured a massive 58cu ft of load space, but it had many new additional trim features as well. One new feature was the protective rubber inserts fitted to front and rear bumpers.

Following on from the FD Victor range, the FE series was introduced in 1972. It came in a number of variants, finally finishing life as the VX1800 and VX2300 models. This particular model was the VX4/90, which had a slightly better turn of speed (101mph as opposed to 95mph of the standard FEs). The VX4/90 also had a number of extra appointments that were not available on the base model, or had to be purchased as 'extra equipment'.

Cavalier 1975-1988

The start of a new breed, and a significant step forward in Vauxhall's modern history, undoubtedly came with one of the most important models of recent times: the all-new Cavalier! But was it an all-new car? Well not really, for this was in actual fact the Opel Ascona, which had hit the streets of Britain in 1974. Yet the Opel did not do well, with just over 1,100 Asconas and 1,700 Mantas (the coupé version) being sold that year. As it was not a staggering success, there were plans to rebadge Belgian-built Opels as Vauxhall models, and a good English name was considered essential.

And what could be more British than the name, Cavalier, so clearly associated with the English Civil War. Well nothing, apart from the fact that the name Cavalier was actually of French origin. Anyway, it was subsequently chosen and it worked well on what has to be considered as a really modern European car, but even so a model that the British really took to heart, albeit retrospectively!

The original Vauxhall Cavalier was introduced in the autumn of 1975 and was initially available in three basic body styles. These were a two-door saloon, a four-door saloon and an attractive two-door coupé. Both of the saloon models were offered with the choice of the 1,600cc or 1,900cc ohc engines, but the two-door coupé was fitted with the 1,900cc engine as standard.

This Mk II Cavalier was recorded in 1989 in the courtyard of my sister Larraine's farmhouse at Caldbeck in Cumbria when it belonged to my brother Michael. Registered in Scotland the car carries a Sapphire Blue metallic paint scheme.

MODEL TYPES

The start of a new breed, and a significant step forward in Vauxhall history, was the introduction of the all-new Cavalier. Stylish, sleek, and with that modern-looking air-dam front end, here we show a basic 1600L two-door saloon model from 1976.

Showing the rear view of the same 1600L saloon featured to the left; this was the first version of a model that was to span a total of three versions and last until 1995 when it was replaced by the Vectra. In fact, the three-millionth Cavalier would be produced in 1993 when the MkIII entered production. From the early beginnings the Cavalier would reach some dizzy heights, with many unusual variations (including a 4x4 model) being produced.

These engines had four cylinders set in line, with the camshaft in the cylinder head. Both the 1,600cc and the 1,900cc had the same piston stroke of 69.8mm. However, the bore diameter of the 1,600 was 85mm, whilst that on the 1,900cc was 93mm; this gave a piston displacement of 1,584cc and 1,897cc respectively. The 1,600cc then produced a maximum of 75bhp at 5,000rpm and the 1,900cc car had 90bhp at 4800rpm. There was also the option of a smaller 1,300cc engine as well, but as these cars were designed to slot into the market between the Viva HC and FE Victor ranges, the 1,256cc engine tended to be overshadowed. It weighed in at 2,489lb (1,290kg) in its GL form, so it needed a fairly substantial power plant. With a 92in (2.52m) wheelbase and an overall length of 175in (4.44m), the Cavalier was 66in (1.67m) wide.

The Cavalier was easily distinguished from the Ascona, as the front of the British-built model had a decidedly different styling. Here, in the steel panel work, a rather tidy slope was achieved to its nose and, like other Luton-built models, it was given what was known as air-dam styling. This was in sharp contrast to the conventional radiator on the Ascona. In the centre of the front panel, between the headlamps, the Cavalier proudly wore the griffin badge. The headlamps were of a rectangular shape, and the whole front end was complemented with a full width, shallow air-intake below the slim chrome bumper. Like the rear bumper, it had a rubbing strip inserted.

When the Cavalier was first shown, Vauxhall curiously seems to have been less than rapturous with its publicity for the model and it was almost as though it was a little afraid that it had got the car wrong. Some thought that the distinctive nose would not find favour with the British public but, as 238,980 MkI models ultimately found buyers, their fears were rather unfounded.

Vauxhall Cars 1965-1984

Registered in the same sequence as the 16L two-door saloon (OVS 49R), this 1900 two-door coupé (OVS 32R) is pictured on the Brache Estate at Luton with the Vauxhall plant behind on 22 July 1976. Curiously the registration sequence was issued in Scotland.

Moving on to the four-door variants, first of all we see one of the modified 1600LS saloons. The changes that came about at the time this model was introduced in the summer of 1980 saw the number of variants on the Cavalier increase to 12.

As mentioned earlier in the text, the original Cavalier was available as both a four-door and two-door saloon. The latter, with a wider door and shorter second side window, tended to have a rather interesting American look. A rather zippy two-door coupé version was produced, and some reviewers said it had a more pleasing style than that of the Firenza body shell. Perhaps this was as a result of the rear side window being almost level and harmonising more with that of the driver's door and the short boot. This was in contrast to the style of the Firenza, with its short side window whose based edge started to rise immediately after leaving the door pillar. It might have been different if the window base had been level or the boot and rear wing line had been level, but this is mere conjecture!

For 1977 the range consisted of the two-door and four-door saloons with a choice of 1,300cc, 1,600cc or 1,900cc engines and the two-door coupé. I suspect that this four-door saloon shown in this late-1977 photograph is one of the new two-litre versions pictured before the upgraded engine came on the market in 1978.

The Firenza was still an extremely good style and deserved to achieve a greater market share than it did, but I digress, except to say that many thought the two-door Cavalier Coupé would succeed where the Firenza had not.

At £2,843 inclusive of Purchase Tax, the Coupé was a true driver's car with a crisp, smooth gear-change, sure-footed directional stability and gave that evocative sensation of being at ease with the machine. A slight increase in weight, approximately 20lb (9.1kg) more than the two-door saloon, was easily handled as this model was usually fitted with the 1,897cc engine. With this power unit, coupled to its distinctive aerodynamic

In 1978 Vauxhall celebrated its 75th anniversary (1903-1978) in some style. The company also witnessed the millionth Bedford van being turned out and the two-millionth Bedford truck. However, the undoubted sales success at the time was the soar-away Cavalier, which was breaking all expectations. Even so, improvements were being planned for 1980 in what would be the last flush of the MkI Cavalier. Here we see a publicity shot of a two-litre GL issued in 1980.

shape, the Coupé could reach a maximum speed of 106mph. Consequently it proved a very popular model even if somewhat marred by a lack of headroom in the rear seats. Another interesting variation of the Coupé was the now rare Centaur convertible.

One thing we have not really mentioned thus far is the subject of seat belts, which had become a legal requirement on all post-1975 cars, and were now a standard fitting. But the fitting of many other accessories was considered as luxury items and became optional extras; for example, a radio on a Cavalier cost £40 in 1975.

In 1978 the Cavalier range was further enlarged when the 2,000cc engine was introduced. Also new was a further body style known as the 'Sportshatch', which was available in 1600 GLS or 2000 GLS variants. As the name suggests, this was a sporting hatchback based on the two-door coupé but now in a true fastback style. From the outset it was offered with a manual or automatic transmission, to complement the entire range of models except those with the 1,256cc engine.

The line up of the first generation of the Vauxhall Cavalier saw the two-door coupé being discontinued during 1979, but the rest of this range of extremely popular saloon cars and their sporting brethren continued in production with periodic cosmetic changes until 1981. The Cavalier had become a serious competitor for the Ford Cortina, but a serious omission to the range was an estate car. This major oversight was not rectified until a MkII estate was produced in 1983.

On 17 August 1981, Ferdie Beickler, who was then Vauxhall's Chairman, drove a white Cavalier saloon off the production line; this was the very first of the second generation Cavalier and is seen in the picture on page 41. This was to be Vauxhall's new model for the 1980s, and there were some radical changes to go with it. These new Cavaliers were powered by four-cylinder 1.3 or 1.6 engines, but these were now mounted transversely at the front driving the front wheels.

Quoting from the press release of the time, this new Vauxhall Cavalier MK1 2000 GLS was a 'top luxury saloon in the Cavalier range, which is readily distinguished from the other models in exterior appearance by its vinyl roof cover!' Tinted glass all round, adjustable front headrest and push-button radio were all included in its extremely full specification.

This transition to front-wheel drive had first been adopted with the Vauxhall Astra, which had been introduced the previous year with the 1.2- and 1.3-litre engines. However, although assembled in Britain, the new Cavalier was a truly global GM car, with parts coming from GM plants in Germany, Belgium, Australia and even Japan!

The new Cavalier had a slightly better range of body styles and was available as a two- or four-door saloon or a five-door hatchback, each with five levels of trim and equipment variations. Opel tended to work more closely with Vauxhall now as opposed to competing with them and, as a result, the Ascona range echoed the Luton cars. The Manta was even sold through Vauxhall dealerships as there was no longer a Vauxhall equivalent.

During 1982 an 1,800cc fuel injection engine was offered in the shape of the 1.8 SRI. This sporty model came with optional two-tone paint, tinted glass, alloy wheels and Recaro seats. The top of the range CD model was also powered by an 1,800cc engine and it had a front spoiler, electric front windows, power steering, velour seats and a five-speed gearbox. Also available at this time was a 1,600cc diesel engine.

As mentioned earlier, 1983 finally saw the introduction of the estate cars. In all four models were offered: the 1600S, 1600S L, and the 1600S GL (all with petrol engines) and the 1600D L diesel-engined model. With the rear seat folded down there was 51cu ft of load space and a load deck height of only 18.1in (45cm), which made loading and unloading far easier. Another feature, now common on many of today's cars, was the

The same press release also included pictures of the GLS Sports Hatch that was introduced for 1981, one of which showed an interior 'driver's eye' view of the cockpit. Note the extremely busy six-dial instrument panel, the short gear-change and the push-button mono-radio/stereo-cassette player.

MODEL TYPES

Left: Externally the MK1 Sports Hatch looked somewhat different from the coupé version introduced back in 1975. For a start the door pillar looks more perpendicular and the rear window obviously longer. Although its parentage is easily discerned, changes to the body shell were on the way, and the new Cavalier MkII would roll off the line within eight months of this picture being taken.

Below: Here we have the first MkII Cavalier to roll off the production line at Luton on 17 August 1981. With bits from GM plants all over the world, this was a really international model.

Above: Carrying a registration plate (VXM 999) that had appeared on publicity pictures of MkI Cavaliers, HC Vivas and the Chevette, this picture — released to the press on 26 August 1981 — shows the rear view of the new MkII Cavalier in its two-door form.

Right: A later variant of the MkII was this hatchback version shown to the press on 14 May 1986. Rejoicing in the name Antibes, the car featured a rubber side moulding and white, stylish wheel hubs — as far as I can recall this model came in a choice of three basic colours, red, white and blue which was a very British colour scheme (or French, Dutch or Norwegian come to that)!

split rear seats, which made it possible to still carry awkward loads and rear seat passengers at the same time. Optional extras were the automatic transmission, metallic paint, stereo radio/cassette player and alloy wheels.

A real surprise was the introduction of a factory-built Cavalier convertible model in 1985, which was based on the two-door saloon with the 1.8-litre injection engine. The boot capacity was reduced to 16.2cu ft because of the storage needed for the all-weather folded hood. Standard features for the convertible included Rallye-twill cloth seat trim, sports front seats with head restraints, stereo radio/cassette, rev-counter, laminated windscreen and electric mirrors. During 1987 a 2.0-litre injection engine was also offered, which meant there was now a choice of four petrol engines or the diesel engine. This also meant that there was now a choice of 14 saloon cars (now only in four-door form), 14 hatchback models, the convertible and five estate cars.

The 1976/77 model Vauxhall Chevette four-door saloon is seen in a pre-release publicity shot that was not to be published until 16 June 1976.

CHEVETTE 1975-1984

After 12 years as one of the leading British small family cars, the ubiquitous Viva was effectively replaced by the Vauxhall Chevette and, along with the larger Astra, it allowed Vauxhall considerably to expand further into the small-car market. The Chevette, which was announced in March 1975, proved to be the last car badged as a Vauxhall that actually used a Vauxhall-designed engine. This was the aforementioned 1,256cc four-cylinder in-line ohv engine, which produced 59bhp at approximately 5,600rpm. Therefore, the new Chevette had a conventional front-engine/rear-wheel drive layout, with transmission through a manual four-speed gearbox.

The Chevette, known as the 'T-Car', was effectively one of GM's world cars. It had first seen the light of day in Brazil in 1974 as a Chevrolet. The 'T-Car' was also sold in the USA, but there it was badged as both Chevrolet and Pontiac versions. The Japanese models used the name Isuzu 1600; this company also supplied engines that powered the Vauxhall Midi vans and minibuses and, of course, West Germany was naturally producing an Opel version.

These German-built models were (unsurprisingly) called the Opel Kadett, but we have found no real conclusive reason for the name used in Britain. One source at Vauxhall said that, as the Chevette was a mini Chevrolet, it was known as the Chev-ette! No doubt someone will be able to tell us the real reason.

The first Chevettes for Britain were the three-door hatchback models introduced at the launch in 1975, followed a year later by the two-door and four-door saloon car versions. Then, by September 1976, an estate car version arrived on the market.

MODEL TYPES

The price of a three-door Chevette L in 1975 was £1,829, which was rather dear for what was then Vauxhall's 'entry market' car. But we have to remember that this was as a result of spiralling inflation (24%) and unprecedented wage rises (27%) at the time, and a real degree of uncertainty in the motor industry. For example, Chrysler-UK had real financial problems, and its share of the British market slipped to a paltry 7%, British Leyland suffered financial collapse and had to be bailed out by the government, and Aston Martin was sold off for a mere £1.05 million.

Although prices were set to rocket, the launch of the Chevette was quite timely, as the energy crisis meant that small cars were a much more practical alternative. Ford would launch its brand new Fiesta the following year, and its price of £1,856 puts the asking price for the Chevette in to true perspective.

When the GM 'T-Car' was initially launched in the UK, it was offered with just two levels of trim, these being the basic model and the L. It was also launched in the very bright colours so typical of the 1970s that, combined with the economy and merits of this new car, gained excellent television and media coverage.

In October 1975 a GL model was announced, and later still came the GLS. Therefore, when the saloons and the estate cars were shown in 1976, the range consisted of four body styles and a choice

Although it was only a small car, the Chevette certainly had ideas above its station in life. It went on to become a very popular family saloon, estate and hatchback, although it was only initially offered as a three-door hatchback when it was launched in 1975. Starting out with a 1,256cc engine, the range was systematically improved and no fewer than 415,608 Chevettes were produced before the model was withdrawn in 1984.

The first of the British Chevettes rolled off the Vauxhall production line on 10 February 1975, an event that was recorded for posterity by the company's Public Relations Department. Once again the distinctive air-dam front end of the car is clearly evident, and echoes of the 'Droopsnoot' Firenza come to mind.

The saloon version of Chevette certainly looked much more conventional as will be seen in this March 1976 picture featuring the two-door Chevette L. This 50mph 50mpg model was certainly seen as a turning point in Vauxhall's fortunes, and in 1976 the company returned towards profitability from a loss of £14 million.

43

Living close to Appleby-in-Westmorland, one gets to see a large number of Vardas on the road during the month of June. This is of course the Romany name for a traditional gypsy caravan, one of which is pictured in the rear of this picture of a new four-door Chevette in 1976. The advent of the four-door saloon and five-door estate really helped Vauxhall's fortunes as it brought the Chevette right into the market place, and there wasn't any lucky heather, clothes pegs or crystal balls in sight.

Above: This 1975 hatchback shows that originally buyers had little option when it came to buying the 1,256cc engined 'T-Car', except for the colour. This particular example was painted red, and had the added luxury of a discreet white coach line down the side. Hardly a 'go-faster' stripe, but if you wished hard enough...

Left: With a top speed of 91mph, the Chevette could quite easily have been graced with that old Vauxhall designation VX4/90. It was a Vauxhall (if you discount the world car concept behind its creation), it had a four-cylinder in line 1,256cc ohv engine and it could do 90mph. Yet it was at the economical business fleet user and families that the new hatchback was squarely aimed. But, despite the initial success of the car, it was obvious that four-door and estate versions would also sell well in the price range of £1,650 to £1,829. The estate thus came to an eager market place in 1976, and an early model is seen here on 22 July 1976.

of four trim levels as there was now the E (economy) model, which did not have the luxury of reclining seats. The L models had bright window surrounds and plaid trim, the GL had a slightly better trim along with a central console, but the GLS models had Velour trim, a centre console and an electric clock. Externally these models also had extra chrome trim, and sports wheels. A very practical 10cwt van version of the estate, called the Chevanne, was also introduced in 1976. It had the estate body shell but with steel side panels to the rear of the front doors instead of glass.

During 1979 a styling change was made to the headlamps, which were now flush fitting as opposed to the previously recessed style. This year also witnessed automatic transmission becoming available on the L and the GL models. Thereafter the range continued basically unchanged, but there were one or two better equipped limited editions that came out to continue customer confidence and support.

MODEL TYPES

The Chevette estate was surprisingly roomy in the back, and with the back seats folded down you could even accommodate a pair of boisterous Golden Labradors. Mind you the single gas-lift door strut was something of a drawback, and when it failed (as those employed on the models used by Alan's firm often did), the tailgate could give you a thump on the back of the head that was as painful as being hit across the shins by a Labrador's tail.

In this April 1975 picture, the potential of the Chevette is being put to the test in the 1975 Economy Test Drive. Supported by a MkI Bedford CF and a Bedford HA van, the Chevette makes a 'pit stop' for refuelling. The fuel and oil sponsors on this particular test were Texaco, as you might guess from the Havoline cans on the van roof.

Vauxhall was also aiming the Chevette at the young driver, who not only wanted an economical car with an initially low purchase price, but also wanted performance. The Chevette came to be perceived as having the novelty of an individual car, which had both personality and at the same time was a little apart from the crowd. To meet these ideals, there came the Command Performance, a special edition three-door hatchback in 1980. The next year, 1981, saw the emergence of the Black Pearl limited edition, which was followed by the Silhouette in 1982.

However, the real sports edition was the Chevette HS, which was in production from 1976 to 1979. In this car Vauxhall packed its 2,300cc engine, which was fitted with 16-valve twin cam heads. These were the cars to aspire to, but as they came with a price tag of £5,317, they were far from the ordinary buyer's reach and were around three times the price of the basic Chevette. In reality the HS was conceived as a rally car first and foremost and what a rally car, for it showed the world that Vauxhall was more than capable of leading the field when it came to the development of a car with true sporting instincts. The HS had come about largely due to the technical genius of Willem 'Bill' Blydenstein, who saw the lazy little Chevette acquire the racing heart of the Magnum and become one of the hottest little hatches around.

Despite the absence of really prominent 'go-faster' stripes, this was the Chevette that really could motor. With a 2,279cc four-cylinder twin overhead cam engine, developing 135bhp, the Chevette 2300 could go 0-60mph in 8½sec. The top speed was 115mph, but the price for the five-speed car was a mere £5,107. The HSR cost £7,146; little wonder that the total build figure was just 450.

The 2300 HS/HSR was in production from 1976 to 1980 but it had little appeal as a road car, although it took second place in the British Rally Car Championship and three other major wins for Pentti Airikkala in its first season.

A HS came home first in the 1978 Mintex International Rally, whilst Dealer Team Vauxhall driver Pentti Airikkala was also first in the 1978 Finland Snow Rally. The fast Finn, Pentti Airikkala, had started racing Vauxhall Magnums but left DTV to rally Ford Escorts, yet was attracted back when the HS arrived on the scene. He achieved Dealer Team Vauxhall's first international success by clinching the Welsh Rally, before going on to establish himself as Vauxhall's leading driver after a superb performance in the British Championship. Other very successful Vauxhall rally drivers included Jimmy McRae, who later joined Opel, Russell Brooks, Will Sparrow, Tony Pond (who achieved five outright victories in just one season) and Derek Bell, who was probably one of the greatest ambassadors of British saloon car racing.

The success of the HS Chevette lay in its overall specifications, but in particular through its well-proven 2.3-litre engine. This engine was given a 16-valve cylinder head, which now produced 135bhp, and was married to a five-speed Getrag gearbox. This was complemented by a more aerodynamic body, which was fitted with glassfibre spoilers.

From this race proven success a further development evolved in the shape of the HSR Chevette, this model had a revised engine that now produced 150bhp. Other noticeable differences were wider wheel arches, wider wheel rims and body side skirts. The HSR also had a different clutch and a revised back axle location.

So, whilst the Vauxhall Chevette probably had more Latin flair than the Viva, thanks to its Brazilian connections, the foreign content of the 'T-Car' concept was largely missed by the British buyers and it proved to be an extremely profitable success story for Vauxhall. It had a great appeal and was very versatile. During its lifespan, from 1975 to 1984, the combined production figures of the hatchback, saloon and estate reached 415,608, whilst 450 of the high performance HS and HSR hatchback models were built.

When Opel launched its Rekord (in a choice of three petrol or one diesel engine options), the car's front-end styling carried a conventional radiator grille. The offering for the British market from Vauxhall was somewhat different, and (in line with styling dictates of the day) the Vauxhall Carlton once more had the air-dam front end. In April 1979 an early Carlton pauses in London during the Trooping Of The Colour.

Carlton 1978-1986

To re-introduce a top-flight car into the Vauxhall range, the company launched its new Carlton model at the 1978 Motor Show. The Carlton was actually based very closely on the Opel Rekord, which had gone into production the previous year, but it still adhered to the proven formula of front-engine/rear-wheel drive. A choice of engine sizes was available, in the form of a 1.8-litre ohc unit, two-litre and 2.2-litre cam-in-head engine, and a 2.3-litre diesel.

Two body styles were available: a four-door saloon and an estate car. All the models were equipped with servo-assisted brakes — disc on the front wheels and drums on the rear — but for added safety the system was dual line, incorporating a special anti-locking valve fitted in the hydraulic line to the rear brakes. Front suspension was of the MacPherson strut system, which was a radical departure from Vauxhall's traditional wishbone type. The rear axle was located by trailing arms and a Panhard rod, and was supported by coil springs and telescopic dampers. Anti-roll bars were fitted at both the front and the rear.

Transmission was through either a four- or a five-speed manual gearbox, but there was also the option of an automatic. The steering gear was of the re-circulating ball type, incorporating a collapsible mesh energy-absorbing steering column.

Styling features were almost identical to the Opel Rekord, but the principal difference in the Carlton models was the reworked front end. This gave an air of individuality for the British market and harmonised perfectly with the Cavalier and Chevette models, thus

Here we see an estate crossing the Thames with Big Ben in the background. For transport scene enthusiasts, in the background are a pair of London's typical black cabs (Austin FX4s), one of the famous AEC Routemaster buses (579 CLT) running on the No 12 service to Dulwich, and an FE model Vauxhall Victor.

giving a degree of family unity to the Vauxhall range. The front end incorporated a similar banked slope to the leading edge of the bonnet that nearly reached down to the simple bumper with its impact strip. A wide air intake was located below the bumper and the headlights were set into the bodywork adjacent to the slope of the bonnet, with turn indicators at their outer edges.

A side-rubbing strip was fitted to the vehicles sides at bumper height, whilst the bumpers themselves had substantial over-riders and door-mounted rear-view mirrors were fitted. Overall length of the Carlton was 186.7in (4.74m) with the estate models being very slightly shorter at 186.3in (4.73m).

The £4,600 car's main competitor was the Ford Granada, and once more it was a market where Vauxhall was playing catch up with its American rivals. In an effort to improve sales, a major face-lift was introduced in 1983, and the Carlton reappeared with a conventional radiator grille. It was still offered as a four-door saloon or as an estate car but now had the choice of three specifications of trim level.

The L was available in either saloon or estate car form, with 1.8- or two-litre petrol engines or 2.3-litre diesel. It was much the same with the GL but without the diesel option! Finally there was the top status model, the CD, but this was only available as a saloon car with the 2.2-litre petrol injection engine. This follows that the estate cars were available as 1800L, 1800GL, 2000L, 2000GL and as a 2300D.

The all-steel bodies on the Carlton were offered with an extensive anti-corrosion treatment as standard, and were available in a choice of 10 solid body colours or eight two-coat metallic colours on the L and GL models. The colours were Brazil Brown, Carmine Red, China Blue, Leaf Green, Mexico Red, Parchment, Polar White, Squadron Blue, Stratos Blue, and black; the metallic colours being Anthracite, Astro Silver, Baryt Brown, Carnelian Red, Helios Blue, Silver Moss, Onyx Brown and White Gold. The 'top flight' Vauxhall at this time, the Carlton CD, had the choice of eight metallic colours, but the choice of solid body colours was limited to Mexico Red, Parchment, Polar White, Stratos Blue, and black. Production of the 1978-1986 Carlton is estimated to have been around 80,000 of all the models.

The Vauxhall Royale Coupé was introduced in 1978 and was the company's first true six-cylinder car since the PC series. Although a six-cylinder had stayed in the range with the FE Ventora, this went out of production in 1976, leaving the FE VX4/90 to carry on as Vauxhall's top of the range car. Customer demand for a larger model in the Vauxhall family stimulated the Royale's emergence, which was available in either saloon or coupé form. However just over 7,000 were eventually built and production was halted in 1982.

ROYALE 1978-1982

The vast number of models to be covered in this book means that we can not give a great deal of space to the next two Vauxhall offerings, but with the Royale came the first six-cylinder Vauxhall since the demise of the Ventora. Aimed squarely against the stylish 3.5-litre Rover SD1 and the Ford Granada Ghia, it carried a 2,784cc in-line engine producing 140bhp inside a body shell originally devised for the Opel Senator/Monza in 1977.

This was to be Vauxhall's *crème-de-la-crème*, and something for the Cavalier buyer to aspire to. The saloon version was based on the Senator but selling for considerably less, for it was priced at £7,956 as opposed to Opel's top-flight luxury car with its 3.0-litre fuel-injection engine which sold for £9,548. Top speed was 115mph, and 0-60mph was reached in a little over 12sec.

Again built to a conventional front-engine/rear-wheel drive layout, it employed a four-speed, all-synchromesh gearbox with the drive through a single dry-plate clutch. However, the General Motors Strasbourg automatic gearbox was an optional choice.

This was Vauxhall's first model to utilise independent suspension all round, with the front having the MacPherson strut system and the rear using coil springs with trailing arms and telescopic dampers. Disc brakes were used both front and rear, and could quickly bring this 3,085lb (1,399kg) of unladen luxurious elegance to a halt!

Fastback two-door coupé models of the Royale (based on the Opel Monza coupé) were also built and had a distinctive broad black-painted door pillar, which formed a strengthening bar. The bumpers incorporated rubber inserts and substantial black rubber over-riders. Overall the saloon cars were 180in (4.57m) long, while the coupe was 185in (4.7m); both were 68in (1.72m) wide. As usual the coupé was slightly lower at 54in (1.37m) as opposed to the saloon's 56in (1.42m). In total 7,119 Royales were built.

This 1980 model Viceroy was not part of a large production batch; in fact fewer than 2,300 were built between 1980 and 1982. Various factors counted against Vauxhall's re-entry into the six-cylinder market, including the established reputation of its competitors. It was also a rapidly shrinking market given the inflationary period that was facing Britain and the spiralling fuel prices as tensions in the Middle East became daily news.

Viceroy 1980-1982

The Viceroy, announced in 1980, proved to be an extremely handsome model, and one that is very easily recognised because of its distinctive fine white cross on the radiator grille (rather after the style of the old FD/FE VX4/90 models). Yet, despite its good looks, this was a curious product for Vauxhall to launch on the market.

Vauxhall already had an enormous range of cars to suit everyone from the economical and compact Chevette and family Astras to the Carlton and rather exclusive Royale, both announced in 1980. As these two models were really designed to fill the customer needs at the upper end of the market, one wonders why Vauxhall thought that it needed the Viceroy to expand them. Admittedly it was more exclusive than the Carlton, and not quite so elegant as the Royale. Again it was an Opel body shell and, if readers closely study the picture shown above, it will be seen that the basic body shell from the front windscreen/bulkhead backwards is actually based on the Opel Rekord. Put into this bits of the Carlton and a front end in keeping with the style of the Royale and you get the Viceroy.

Only one body style was offered on the Viceroy throughout its 1980-1982 production span: a four-door saloon. Similarly it only came with one power unit — a straight six engine of 2,490cc fitted with a Zenith twin choke carburettor — and a four-speed all-synchromesh gearbox. In yet another big car, a conventional front-engine/rear-wheel drive layout was employed. Standard equipment featured central locking, stereo radio cassette player and velour upholstery. Later models had the feature of black side window surrounds and a striped trim. The 1980 cost of the Viceroy was £7,864 compared to the Carlton's £4,600; even so a total of 2,295 were built before production finished in 1982!

Vauxhall's luxury car for the early 1980s, the Senator.

SENATOR 1984-1987

Obviously, it was a pointless and confusing exercise to have so many top of the range cars on the go at the same time, and in 1982 common sense prevailed. Rationalisation of the Opel and Vauxhall ranges saw a new top car, the Senator. Until October 1984 this was only badged as an Opel model, but then Vauxhall got its very own high-specification executive model. Badge engineering or not, this was one of the finest cars in its class available in Europe. It had a wheelbase of 105.6 (2.68m) and an overall length of 190.5in (4.84m), so it was not small. In fact it was 48in (1.21m) longer than a Nova and packed from stem to stern with luxury.

Available in the four-door saloon format only, it had a choice of three models: a 2.5-litre and a 3.0-litre saloon or the top-flight 3.0-litre Senator CD. These cam-in-head six-cylinder engines had electronic ignition (with electronic ignition timing), hydraulic tappets, viscous drive cooling fan and 12 crankshaft counter-balanced weights; in addition, the three-litre engine also featured a thermostatically-controlled engine oil cooler.

External styling was important and a feature of the Senator was the front bumper with integral spoiler, which contributed so much to the cars 'straight-line stability'. It had bright trim on all the window perimeters. There were black side-window surrounds on the CD, whilst those on the other two models were in body colour.

The interior specification was lavish, especially in the CD, with such features as velour cloth seat trim and door panels, carpeted load compartment, height-adjustable and electrically-heated front seats, air-conditioning, an adjustable steering wheel, liquid crystal display instrumentation, a seven-function trip computer, digital clock, headlamps-on warning buzzer, illuminated locking glove box, integral map reading lights, illuminated vanity mirror, a continental-style front door arm rest... and the list went on.

The three-door Astra hatchback was yet another standardised product, which sold all over Europe as the Opel Kadett. In 1983 the GTE version was launched, and this had an immediate impact on the 'hot hatchback' market. From 1984 to 1991 a MkII version was built.

ASTRA MkI 1980-1984

After so many years at the forefront of the British family car market, the Vauxhall Viva was withdrawn from production in 1979. Yet, no-one could complain as HC models had been in production for a full decade and 640,863 had been built. The car that took its place for 1980, the Astra, was a major departure from Vauxhall's traditional four-cylinder in-line engines and rear-wheel drive. The new Astra featured transverse engines and front-wheel drive!

The Astra was first publicly shown at the Scottish Motor Show held at the Kelvin Hall in Glasgow, as there was no Motor Show at Earl's Court in 1979. Once again this 'new' Vauxhall was actually based on a German car, the Opel Kadett. The Astra was intended to sell between the top-priced Chevette and the lowest-priced Cavalier, thus meaning that the Viva range had actually been superseded by two types of vehicle and this helped to expand the market for the Astra in both directions. It was produced as a three- or five-door hatchback or a three- or five-door estate car, although not all the variants were offered at first.

The first engine options offered on the Astra were also German power plants (from the Opel Kadett) but there was little performance difference, as these were a 1.2-litre and a 1.3-litre engine. Both engines had four-cylinders in line, but were mounted transversely to give front-wheel drive. The 1,196cc unit had a bore and stroke of 79mm x 61mm, and produced 60bhp at 5,800rpm. Meanwhile the 1,297cc engine had an almost square configuration, with the cylinder bore being 75mm and a piston stroke of 73.4mm; this resulted in 75bhp at 5,800rpm.

These were belt-driven overhead camshaft engines with hydraulic tappets, using a cast-iron cylinder block with an aluminium cylinder head and a five-bearing crankshaft.

MODEL TYPES

Transmission for the Vauxhall Astra was by a four-speed all-synchromesh manual gearbox, although there was once again the option of having an automatic gearbox. However, some of the contemporary reviews of the Astra accused the car of having a less than smooth gear change and being underpowered. During 1981 a larger engine size was offered in the shape of a 1,598cc petrol engine, which produced 90bhp. This was the 'J-Car' GM power train, which had been developed as part of the World Cars programme and intended for the Opel Ascona and the first generation of the Vauxhall Cavalier. The clever thinking behind the World Car concept was undoubtedly the brainchild of some accounting programme, but was it a practical way forward?

Eric Dymock (the *Sunday Times*' motoring correspondent) stated in his useful little handbook *The Vauxhall File*: 'the series of "world" cars [was] inspired by the accountants of mega-manufacturers, but [was] rarely endorsed by "world" customers.' Even so the new 1.6-litre engine was a marked improvement, and it showed in the reviews of the day. It dispensed with the cam-in-head design (by then approaching 17 years old), and also did away with the rockers.

This was now a real overhead cam engine, in which the valves were worked by cantilever followers. The two-piece aluminium cylinder head was also a clever piece of engineering, with the upper part being a pressure die-cast unit. Unlike many of the transverse engines of the time, it had the benefit of diagonal combustion chambers. It was a fairly light engine too, weighing in at about 55lb (24kg) less than its predecessor. A further feature was in the distributor, which was driven off the overhead camshaft, but this initially caused teething problems in some of the early Cavaliers. Yet, with this power unit in the Vauxhall Astra, the 1.6 GTE became one of the hottest little hatchbacks around in 1983.

Mind you, not content with the improvement in the petrol engine, GM was also keen to improve performance and couple this with economy. In Germany the new Corsa was selling well, and its British equivalent — the Nova — would have been launched but for industrial problems with the British unions. The Nova was envisaged as taking some of the lower end of the Astra market, allowing it to move up a notch. Now, this was to be achieved with the more powerful engines, better appointments and some cosmetic changes, but already the 'T-85' programme was well under way. The 'T-85' would see the second generation Astra, with its superb aerodynamic styling resulting in a low coefficient of drag (CD factor). This was then seen as being almost as important as the high power to weight ratio that had previously been considered all-important.

An Astra three-door hatchback. Unfortunately we have no firm indication of the engine size on this particular car, but from the fact that it carries metallic paint and has front seat head rests, I would suggest that this is a 1600GL which was a new model for 1981.

All right, OUR 109W is not a yellow 1200S E type Astra, it is a red Astra 1300S GL model! Just to confuse future historians, the PR Department decided to throw a few spanners in the works. Maybe they were trying to fool Ford, Chrysler and British Leyland, but they sure as anything succeeded with us.

Nevertheless, until the MkII Astra appeared, the new 1,600cc diesel engine and an even more powerful 1,800cc petrol engine were seen as a way of further expanding the list of options. However, the new diesel engine was an outstanding contribution to the Astra range, and therefore merits some further mention. Whilst not dissimilar to the second-generation four-cylinder 1.6-litre ohc petrol engine, there were a number of notable differences. The main ones were an aluminium cylinder head, connecting rods produced from reinforced cast-iron and a Ricardo Comet V combustion chamber. This new GM engine had been revealed at the Brussels Motor Show, as the demand for diesel-powered cars had grown steadily in Europe.

In Britain there was only an anticipated demand for about 10,000 diesel cars, but politics were to play a significant part in the state of affairs within the motor industry in 1983. It was a hard time for many motor manufacturers, and both Lotus and DeLorean were in serious trouble, and even the giant of British motoring Dunlop Tyres was sold to the Japanese firm Sumitomo. The Conservatives under Margaret Thatcher had been in power for four years, and despite the decimation of traditional British industries under the 'Iron Lady', there was a general 'feel good factor' at play. Those who had lost out — such as the coal miners, the steel workers and the like who may not agree — but there was a great degree of optimism in the British car industry. To persuade voters to give them another term, the Tories sharply reduced taxes in the annual Budget as a sweetener for the forthcoming election.

As far as motoring was concerned, the Chancellor of the Exchequer played his trump card, but it was also one that suited Vauxhall very well indeed. This came about when he announced three new taxation classes: up to 1.3-litre, 1.3-litre to 1.8-litre and over 1.8-litre. Vauxhall's Astra range neatly fitted into two of these brackets, and plans to drop the 1.2-litre model in the MkII range were suddenly abandoned. The 1.8-litre versions of both Astra and Cavalier gave Vauxhall a distinct advantage over the other big fleet car supplier, Ford, who found itself having to produce a 1.8-litre version of its cars to stay in the running.

MODEL TYPES

Now this is a little simpler to identify, for here we have a fairly easy car to caption, for this is one of the four-door estates that were brought into Britain in 1979 ahead of the Astra debut. As there was no Earl's Court Motor Show that year, the Astra was launched at the Scottish Motor Show held in Kelvin Hall, Glasgow. Oddly, but in line with current GM policy of the time, Opel also promoted the almost identical Kadett at the same show.

Just for a slightly different perspective on the OUR-W registration plate sequence, we now see OUR 112W on a two-door version of the Astra estate. Carrying the 1300S badging, this L model was finished in metallic blue paint. The same body shell, with solid sides instead of rear windows, was used quite successfully as an economical light commercial.

    In Europe, a big political issue was being expressed in environmental concerns, both in terms of pollution and (more importantly) energy-saving. Accordingly the diesel engine and new 'lead free petrol' engines were set to become an increasingly important part of the future.

    In the terms of styling and design, the MkI Astra missed the mark a little, but as a practical, economical and reliable form of transport it cannot be criticised. Its features may have been a little bland, but there was nothing ugly about it or even anything out of proportion. It had a tidy black radiator grille set on its prow, with just enough fine chrome to get it noticed. A small air spoiler incorporated into the bodywork was located just below the almost plain black bumper, whilst the nearly square headlights had just enough slope to them to harmonise with the camber of the radiator grille. It carried 155x13 pressed steel wheels (shaped like a fallen pepper pot), with eyebrow wheel arches to the bodywork above.

    The structure of the body shell was very neat and tidy, but nothing really exciting although Vauxhall did challenge this train of thought for 1983. In that year the company brought it up to date, with the announcement of the sporty three-door GTE model. This had front and rear spoilers, wheel arch and sill extensions, a five-speed gearbox, tinted glass and Recaro seats and gave the Vauxhall Astra a whole new image. Other variations on the Astra were the Astramax van and a van-based estate car, both of which useful additions to the range giving car performance coupled with a greatly increased carrying capacity.

    The Vauxhall Astra was of integral steel construction, with independent front suspension of MacPherson struts with coil springs and anti-roll bar. The rear suspension had trailing arms with torsional crossbeam and coil springs, and again an anti-roll bar. The braking system was the traditional and well-proven layout of disc brakes at the front and drum brakes on the rear. The MkI reached the end of its production life in 1984 when the model was superseded by the Astra II, which carried on the name until 1993. However, a production life of 13 years was not unlucky for the Astra because an extremely impressive total of 1,117,662 vehicles had been produced by 1993.

55

When General Motors launched its 'World Car' concept, its 'T-Car' model came to Britain in the shape of the successful Chevette. When this was expanded to the 'S-Car' the company envisaged few major problems, but an industrial dispute delayed this model's introduction on to the British market. Once the stumbling blocks were resolved, the new Vauxhall Nova hit the streets in 1983. It went on to become such a popular and successful car, that nearly half a million (446,462) were built before production ended in 1993.

Nova 1983-1993

As mentioned previously, the new taxation classes announced in the 1983 budget played straight into the hands the manufacturers of small cars and, at the time, Vauxhall enjoyed a major share of this market in Britain. It was a period of change in this country, for in addition to the wearing of seat belts becoming compulsory, it had already reached the time when registration numbers would change. Now the 'year' letter would prefix the registration, in the form of A123 XYZ. For salesmen this meant a bonanza, as people rushed to be ahead of the crowd (or more importantly their neighbours) by owning a new 'A Reg' car.

Yet the competition in new cars was not all that hot, British Leyland had the new LM10 (the Maestro) to replace the Allegro (all agro), Daihatsu launched the new 30bhp Domino, Fiat threw the Uno at an unsuspecting British public, Ford prided itself on the 'big small car' (the Orion), the Lada Riva came out as a much modified form of the Fiat 124, Peugeot offered the 205 hatchback, and Vauxhall gave Britain the Nova.

The design brief for the new GM 'S-Car' stated simply 'make this the finest all-round small car in Europe', and when it was finished the result met all the demanding requirements that its design team had set out to achieve. Despite union problems delaying its introduction, Vauxhall was justifiably proud to receive the following endorsement from a review in *Autosport*: 'What is so impressive about the Nova is that at their first attempt General Motors have got it exactly right.' Although GM was late developing a 'super mini', it now had a new compact car to compete in the same market as the Renault 5, Fiat 127, Nissan Micra, Volkswagen Polo and the Ford Fiesta!

MODEL TYPES

When originally introduced this little car was available with either a 1.0-, a 1.2- or a 1.3-litre engine in the modern transversely-mounted front-engine/front-wheel drive layout. Two body styles were offered at first: a three-door hatchback and a two-door saloon. To protect the body of the car, the all-steel construction was given an extensive anti-corrosion treatment. Meanwhile, to protect the bodies inside the car, there were front and rear crumple zones with a rigid passenger safety cell. The saloon had pronounced wheel arches, but the styling of the hatchback incorporated a horizontal ridge in a shallow crescent style a short distance above the plain wheel arch.

Development, as with all of the Vauxhall range, was centred around a philosophy of continual commitment to ever-increasing improvement. Therefore (by 1985), as well as having the choice of the two body styles and four- or five-speed gearbox on the two smaller engines, the 1.3-litre was available with five-speed as standard. Four levels of specification were offered, these being the basic Nova, the Nova L, the GL model and then the top of the range SR (which was only available in hatchback form). All models had fully reclining front seats, but the SR had sports seats and also the Daytona check trim. Externally the SR's recognisable features included sports wheels (with low profile tyres), a front sports spoiler and a tailgate spoiler.

Even at entry-level, the Nova had a surprising level of comfort, for a start the seats were upholstered in a cloth trim called Domino (rather than the accursed vinyl of earlier basic Vauxhalls). The front seats also had 'see through' head restraints, a boot mat in the saloon (load floor mat in the hatchback), a full-width front parcel shelf and a lidded glove box, whilst the front doors were fitted with armrests.

In line with GM's World Car Concept of that time, Vauxhall found itself having to say Viva Espania, when it was directed to import the 'S-Car' from the GM plant in Spain. Initially there was considerable resistance from the unions, and perhaps understandably so, as Vauxhall were then enjoying around 12% of the UK car market. Once the dispute was settled, the two-door model began to appear under the Vauxhall brand name Nova.

Initially intended as a rival to the Ford Fiesta and the Volkswagen Polo, the Nova came in three engine sizes, one-litre, 1.2 and 1.3; later on a 1.5 diesel and a 1.6 petrol engine were added to the range. Here is a Nova 1.3 GL saloon publicity view from 1984.

57

Externally all Novas had Halogen headlamps as standard and thermoplastic bumper covers, while all but the base Nova had body-side protection mouldings fitted. All Novas had laminated windscreens but the three more expensive models also had bronze tinted glass and a windscreen tint shade band. They also came equipped with a locking fuel cap, reversing light, fog lamp, hazard warning lights and a heated rear window, two-speed windscreen wipers with intermittent wipe; the tailgate on the hatchback also had the intermittent wash and wipe.

It is also worth mentioning that even in a small compact, all the Nova models had the benefit of an electric front screen wash, with the three premium models having a retractable aerial and remote-control driver's mirror. The rear seats were now of the split 60/40 pattern on the L models upwards.

During 1985 the base, L, and GL Novas were available in a choice of seven solid colours: Brazil Brown, Carmine Red, China Blue, Leaf Green, Parchment, Polar White or, at an extra cost, black. Also available was a choice of four two-coat metallic colours: Astro Silver, Carnelian Red, Onyx Brown and Silver Moss. The SR models were available in Astro Silver and five solid body colours: Brazil Brown, Carmine Red, Jamaica Yellow, Polar White and black.

For the 1985 season the Nova range was extended with a five-door hatchback, a four-door saloon and a special edition saloon called the Merit. By 1987 there were seven saloon cars and 10 hatchbacks and, if you think carefully about this fact, you may consider that it was quite remarkable that such a wide choice was given in what was, after all, only the entry-level market.

In a pre-launch picture issued on 29 April 1983, we see a Nova 1.2L from the rear aspect. This picture was actually taken in the late summer or early autumn of 1982, and a very summery scene is conjured up from the tennis players in the background.

A facelift was given to the Nova in 1986, and the new Antibes hatchback was launched to the public in April that year. However, as these styling changes had been conceived in 1984, we thought it worthy of including a picture of one of these 'style-editions' in this book. This Nova 1.2 Antibes dates from early in 1985.

MODEL TYPES

Although beyond the scope of this book, it is worth mentioning that during the mid-1980s Vauxhall was experimenting with new safety features for the second half of the decade. As an example, for reasons of durability and environmental safety, the company revealed that by 1987 the Nova's rear brake linings would be absolutely asbestos free. Another safety aspect was the fitting of three rear seat belts (two inertia belts and a central lap-belt). Engineering improvements during this time included the now standard fitting of a 55amp alternator to ensure full efficiency of the battery.

Finally, it should mentioned that in 1988 a new sporting model made its way into the limelight, with the Nova GTE with a 1,600cc petrol-injection engine producing 100bhp. This potent little beast was given stiffer suspension, a close-ratio five-speed gearbox and larger steel wheels. It could also reach speeds approaching 117mph. During the 10 years of the Nova's production life 446,462 cars were built in both saloon and hatchback models before it was withdrawn in 1993.

Top: Taking this book into the next period 1985-2004 is problematical to say the least, but as car production on many models did not cease at the time we chose for our break-off date, we are, therefore, obliged to show the continuation of some models beyond the time span being discussed. In the last book this resulted in the PC Cresta being included, although its launch date was actually not until 1965. In this book we will give brief consideration to how the Nova continued into the next period. In 1985 an all-new body style appeared, and a smart GTE version arrived. In 1986 an SRi version was launched and a two-litre came the following year. In 1987 a 1.5-litre diesel engine version was launched. Here we see one of the new GTE hatchbacks pictured early in 1988.

In one of its final guises, the Nova GSi is seen on 7 January 1992.

The Concept Cars

In every industry it is important to realise that appearances relate to successful sales, the first visual contact with any commodity, be it food, fashion, or furnishings, is the first selling point. This law is all the more crucial in the highly competitive car industry and to this end car manufacturers either use their own or independent styling houses. Obviously names like Sir Alec Issigonis (creator of the Mini), Franco Scaglione (Lamborghini), Rod Mansfield (Ford) and David Jones (Vauxhall), should need no introduction to the roles they played in design and styling matters.

Often the task of creating any new car came first with its styling, as the look of the car is often initially considered more important than its mechanical development. As we have already seen, power plants, gearboxes, transmissions and a whole host of smaller components could span several model ranges. In some cases even cars of today use items that were first designed many years ago, and engine blocks are a good example of 'long-lived' pieces of design technology.

Therefore, styling designers would have a good basis on what componentry they could use, and thus they often concentrated on the look of the thing. This meant producing detailed scale drawings, wooden scale models and even full-size clay models in order to incorporate new styling features and thereby analyse advantages, iron out problems and make production as cost effective as possible. All this helped to keep the eventual sales price down.

Of course not every design would work out, and some ideas were taken into manufacturing stages as a 'Concept Car', but never put into full production. The idea behind these concept cars was to test reaction, help with forward planning and also act as the test bed for ideas that could be incorporated in other production models.

Was this really a Vauxhall car conceived in the 1960s? Well yes it was, and with shades of something from TV's *Thunderbirds*, *Captain Scarlet* or *Joe 90*, this was the XRV. Displayed at the Earl's Court Motor Show in 1970, this stunning good looker was to survive into the 21st century (in which its 'futuristic looks' really belong) as it is now part of Vauxhall's Heritage Collection based at Luton. This concept car enjoyed several aerodynamic aids, which even then were only just starting to make an appearance in Formula One racing cars. It also had a reinforced glass-fibre and carbon-fibre body.

THE CONCEPT CARS

Two Vauxhall might-have-beens in the shape of concept cars designed in the 1960s. Above we show the sporty SRV car from 1966 and below the XRV, which was eventually constructed in 1970.

61

Vauxhall Cars 1965–1984

Vauxhall was no different; in fact it was far better than most, thanks to David Jones and his team. One of his most stunning concept cars — the XVR — was shown to the public at the Geneva Motor Show in 1966. This bright orange car had been designed and constructed at Vauxhall's Engineering & Design Centre. Some of the other offerings from the Vauxhall Styling Department are shown in this section.

Also futuristic for its time was the SVR conceived by David Jones and his styling team at Luton in the mid-1960s. It was thought of as being a 'future trend in world design', but doesn't the car have something of the look of the American GM Corvette. It was designed to combine speeds of over 100mph, with front-rank handling, and a high degree of driver and passenger safety! It also had great comfort driver levels, despite the very low overall height. Launched at the 1966 Geneva Motor Show the car never went into full production, but it too became part of the Vauxhall Heritage Collection. It had a four-cylinder 1,595cc ohv engine, but the design study did not include engine specifications, so the final choice of power unit (had it gone into production) could have been much different. It had Goodyear low-profile cross-ply tyres on 13in diameter rims. Only this single model was ever built. Incidentally the name SRV stood for Styling Research Vehicle.

In this publicity shot dated 14 October 1971, we see a superb view of the Costin Amigo. The young chap in the picture must now be in his forties, and would probably wish this sleek two-seater was his today. It was not really a concept car, but as only eight were built we have included it here for the sake of completeness. It had Victor mechanics, a 1,975cc engine, and could achieve in excess of 130mph. Yet, remarkably (like the Marcos Volvo) it had a wooden chassis. It was designed by Frank Costin, whose name was heavily associated with the Marcos brand.

THE CONCEPT CARS

The styling and design department at Vauxhall had seen some notable achievement under David Jones, and later Wayne Cherry, but it was closed down in 1980 when the function was transferred to Germany. It was fitting then that the last all-British design to come out of Luton was something special. The 1978 concept car, the Equus, was also the first open sports car built by the company since the 1930s, as all the other 'cabriolet' versions that had appeared in between were adaptations of standard saloons. The Equus was conceived as a possible contender into a market that MG had dominated for many years, but it was an uncertain market and even then MG was seriously under considerable difficulties. Presumably the hierarchy decided that it was a concept that should not be pursued, and just this single 2,279cc car was produced. It was finished in metallic silver paint, and had a dark blue leather interior complemented by red plush carpeting.

Index

Vauxhall models
Astra...........40, 42, 50, 52, 53, 54, 55
Astramax.........................55
Bedford Beagle 6
Carlton 47, 48, 50
Carlton GL........................48
Carlton 1800L 48
Carlton 1800GL...................48
Carlton 2000L 48
Carlton 2000GL...................48
Carlton 2300L 48
Cavalier 26, 34, 36, 38, 39, 40,
              41, 47, 49, 52, 53, 54
Cavalier 1600 GLS 39
Cavalier 2000 GLS 39
Cavalier Coupé...............38, 39
Cavalier Centaur 39
Cavalier 1600S 40
Cavalier 1600S L 40
Cavalier 1600S GL 40
Cavalier 1600D L 40

Chevanne..........................44
Chevette 42, 45, 47, 50
Chevette Black Pearl.............45
Chevette Command Performance 45
Chevette E 44
Chevette GL 43, 44
Chevette GLS 43
Chevette HS/HSR 45, 46
Chevette L 43, 44
Chevette Silhouette..............45
Corsa.............................53
Cresta/Velox PA 6
FB Victor 7
FC Victor Deluxe Estate...........8
FC Victor Deluxe 8
FC Victor Estate 8
FC Victor Standard 8
FC Victor Super 8, 18
FC Victor VX4/90 ....7, 8
FC Victor 7
FC101 Victor 17

FD Victor VX4/90 ....19, 20, 30, 50
FD Victor 15, 17, 20, 22, 24
FE Estate 24
FE Victor VX4/90....32, 33, 34, 35, 50
FE Victor......................32, 33, 34, 37
FE Victor SL 32, 33
FE Victor Estate 32, 33
Firenza HP Coupé
  'Droopsnoot'....................29, 30
Firenza 24, 27, 29, 38
F-Type Victor.....................6
HA Viva 6
HA90 Viva 6
HB Viva 160 12
HB Viva Brabham 12, 15, 30
HB Viva Deluxe 10, 15
HB Viva GT 15
HB Viva SL 10, 12, 15
HB Viva................4, 6, 10, 15, 18, 23
HB90 10
HC Viva Deluxe 24

63

Vauxhall Cars 1965-1984

HC Viva SL 24
HC Viva Standard 24
HC Viva 23, 24, 26, 27, 30, 31,
37, 42, 46, 52
Magnum Coupé 27
Magnum estate 30
Magnum 31, 45, 46
Midi van 52
Monza Coupé 4
Nova 3, 4, 51, 53, 56, 57, 58
Nova GL 57, 58
Nova GTE 59
Nova L 57, 58
Nova Merit 58
Nova SR 57, 58
PC Cresta Deluxe 9
PC Cresta 9, 10
PC Viscount 9
PC 4
Royale 49, 50
Senator 4, 51
Senator CD 51
Ten-Four 6
Ventora 20, 32, 34, 49
Viceroy 50
Victor 2000 18
Victor 3300 .... 19, 20
Viva E Coupé 27
VX1800 .... 34, 35
VX2300/VX2300 GLS 34, 35
XVR 62

Airikkala, Pentti 46
Aston Martin 43
Austin 20
Autosport 56
BARC hill climb 13
Beickler, Ferdie 39
Blydenstein, Willem 12, 13, 45
BMC Maxi 23
BMC 20, 21
Borg & Beck clutch 10, 19, 29
Borg Warner transmission 10
Brabham, Jack 15
British Championship 46
British Leyland 43
British Leyland Allegro 56
British Leyland Marina 34
British Leyland Maestro (LM10) 56
Brooks, Russell 46
Brussels Motor Show 54
Chevrolet 19, 42
Chrysler 21, 43
Crayford 12
Dagenham 21
Daihatsu Domino 56

David Brown Gears 26
David Brown Tractors 26
DeLorean 54
Domino trim 57
Don Safety Trophy 18
Donnelly, Des 12
Dryden, Bill 12
Dymock, Eric 53
Dunlop 54
Earl's Court 52
Ellesmere Port 24
Fiat 124 56
Fiat 127 56
Fiat Uno 56
Fine Fare Supermarkets 12
Finland Snow Rally 46
Ford Capri 27, 29, 30
Ford Cortina 34, 39
Ford Escort 46
Ford Fiesta 43, 56
Ford Granada/Granada Ghia 48, 49
Ford MkII 1.6 Cortina 12
Ford MkIII Cortina 23, 24, 26
Ford MkIV Zephyr 21
Ford Orion 56
Ford Zodiac 21
Ford 26, 54, 60
Getrag gearbox 46
Girling 8, 10
GM gearbox 9
GM Ricardo Comet V 54
GM 'J-Car' 53
GM 'S-Car' 56
GM 'T-Car' 43, 46
Granada 12
Halogen headlamps 58
Hillman Avenger 23
Hillman Hunter 21
ICI 26
Issigonis, Sir Alec 60
Isuzu 1600 42
Jones, David 9, 10, 32. 60, 62
Kelvin Hall, Glasgow 52
Lada Riva 56
Lamborghini 60
Laycock de Normanville 19
Leyland 21
Lotus 54
Luton 4, 24, 37, 40
MacPherson strut 47, 49, 55
Mansfield, Rod 60
Marshall, Gerry 12
McDougall's Flour 12
McRae, Jimmy 46
Millbrook 24
Mini 60

Mintex International Rally 46
Morris Oxford 21
Nissan Micra 56
Opel 46, 51
Opel Ascona 36, 37, 40, 53
Opel Kadett 10, 42, 52
Open Manta 36, 40
Opel Monza 49
Open Rekord 47, 50
Opel Senator 34, 49
Osram/GEC championship 13
Panhard 47
Paris Motor Show 23
Peugeot 205 56
Pond, Tony 46
Pontiac 42
Porsche 1699SC 9
Powerglide gearbox 9
Radio Rentals 12
Recaro seats 40
Renault 5 56
Rootes 21
Rover SD1 49
Rostyle wheels 19, 30, 35
Scaglione, Franco 60
Scottish Motor show 52
Solex PSEI-7 carburettor 10
Sparrow, Will 46
Stork Margarine 12
Strasbourg gearbox 18, 49
Stromberg Carburettor 6, 10, 29
Sumitomo 54
Sunday Times 53
'T-85' 53
Thatcher, Margaret 54
Thompson, Jim 12
Triumph 1300/1300TC 23
Triumph 1500 23
Triumph 21, 22
Vauxhall 4, 8, 10, 51, 57, 59, 60
Vauxhall File, The 53
Volkswagen Polo 56
Volvo 123 22
Volvo 140 22
Welsh Rally 46
World Cars 53
Zenith 19, 50
ZF gearbox 29